I HAD TO SAY SOMETHING

I HAD TO SAY SOMETHING

THE ART OF TED HAGGARD'S FALL

MIKE JONES

with SAM GALLEGOS

SEVEN STORIES PRESS

New York ▪ London ▪ Melbourne ▪ Toronto

Seven Stories Press
140 Watts Street
New York, NY 10013
www.sevenstories.com

In Canada: Publishers Group Canada, 559 College Street, Suite 402, Toronto, ON M6G 1A9

In the UK: Turnaround Publisher Services Ltd., Unit 3, Olympia Trading Estate, Coburg Road, Wood Green, London N22 6TZ

In Australia: Palgrave Macmillan, 627 Chapel Street, South Yarra, VIC 3141

College professors may order examination copies of Seven Stories Press titles for a free six-month trial period. To order, visit www.sevenstories.com/textbook or send a fax on school letterhead to (212) 226-1411.

Book design by Jon Gilbert

Library of Congress Cataloging-in-Publication Data

Jones, Mike (Michael Forest)
  I had to say something : the art of Ted Haggard's fall / Mike Jones ; with Sam Gallegos. -- 1st ed.
     p. cm.
  ISBN-13: 978-1-58322-768-8 (hardcover)
  ISBN-10: 1-58322-768-7 (hardcover)
 1. Sexual misconduct in clergy--United States. 2. Clergy--Sexual behavior.
 3. Clergy--Deposition. 4. Haggard, Ted. 5. Jones, Mike (Michael Forest)
 I. Gallegos, Sam. II. Title.

BV4392.5.J66 2007
261.8'35766092--dc22
[B]
                                                  2007015845
Printed in the U.S.A.

9 8 7 6 5 4 3 2 1

To the best friend I ever had, my golden girl, my mom

CONTENTS

◨

PREFACE

Let me begin by saying that I do not hate Ted Haggard. I have not rejoiced in what has happened to him. I did not throw a party or dance in the street when he resigned. I was truly sad. It is a much bigger sin in the evangelical movement to be a homosexual than an addict. That's why it would have been harder for Ted Haggard to admit to having gay sex with me than to admit to having a drug problem. Ted is not a mean or vicious person. He is a gentle man and was kind and generous with me. Ted has done some good work in the community. He cares about the environment. I am sure he gave hope to many people who were in despair. I want to believe that he is a good father to his children. He, like me and everyone else, is human. We all have faults, emotions, needs, and wants. I have cried many nights, and I am sure Ted has, too. But this is not what this story is about. Ted believes that the homosexual part of his life is "repulsive and dark." I can tell you that I and my gay friends do not consider ourselves "repulsive." We are not ashamed. You must not speak out against something that you do in secret. You must practice what you preach. Let us not forget that the ultimate word in this story is *hypocrisy*.

—Denver, March 2007

CHAPTER I

ART FROM KANSAS CITY

"Hi, Mike, it's Art from Kansas City."

Within minutes, the man with the light brown hair lay naked on my massage table. Silhouetted by the light from just one candle, he lay on his stomach with his arms at his sides. The room was quiet except for the sounds of the ocean playing in the background. His breathing was muted and his movement was limited. He was both excited and nervous about what was going to happen.

I stepped from behind the curtain that separated the kitchen from the rest of the studio apartment. Naked, I walked over to a table of supplies I kept in the corner of the room. Taking a few squirts of unscented massage lotion, I walked over to Art and stood in front of him, with his head just an inch away from my crotch. I never used scented lotions, since the last thing a client needed was to walk out smelling like he'd been somewhere he shouldn't have gone. I leaned over him and began rubbing the massage lotion into his lower back. As I extended my arms, my groin was right at his head as it lay in the face cradle of the table. Art put one hand on each buttock and gently began rubbing my legs.

Instead of the ocean, the room was now filled with the soft sounds of relaxation music. The room was dark but gave off an air of freshness and cleanliness.

I continued to rub sensually, moving my hands up and

down his back. "How's that feel, handsome?" I asked in a whisper.

He said nothing, instead letting out a soft moan of pleasure, trying to pull me into his face. Feeling my groin pressing against his head, he lifted his head out of the cradle and pressed against me, making sure his forehead, eyes, nose, mouth, and chin all came in contact with my body. I continued to rub his back with a light, Swedish-massage touch. From previous sessions, I knew he enjoyed being touched everywhere, so working a particular muscle was not as important.

He was clearly getting turned on, yet he still seemed unsure of what he could do or how far he wanted to go. I could tell that he wanted to try a lot of things with me but just could not let himself do it. There was hesitancy there. By touching him more sensually than sexually in certain areas, I hoped to get him to feel a bit more comfortable. As I massaged his back, I initially steered clear of his butt.

He wanted to make love to me and to have some sort of intimate connection. Yet there was a line there that he could not cross, and I did not want to push him past that line until he was ready. I massaged his shoulder blades and then worked my way up his arms. I rubbed his hands, which were still placed firmly on my buttocks. Rather than massage each individual finger, I placed my hands on his hands, pushing his fingers deeper into my glutes. His face still rubbing my crotch, he moaned with pleasure.

I took his hands off my ass and put my hands under his arms so he could flip over. Once on his back, I saw, just as I suspected, that he was turned on. I moved to the side of the massage table where he could touch me easily. As he lay there, his eyes were closed and his body was tense.

"That feels so good!" he exclaimed as I touched him. His

head moved from side to side, just like his body tried to. His body language told me when he wanted to play some more, that he had not yet reached a point where the next thing he wanted was release.

"What would you like to do now, handsome?" I whispered.

Art said nothing but guided my hand to his groin. Focusing on the touch, I massaged his groin with simple motions, just the way he liked it.

"Mike, that feels so good!" His body was getting tenser. For a man, that's good.

I played with him a little more until I felt him pulsating. Releasing my grip a bit, I let nature do the rest. And within moments, everything was over. Art did not like to be touched once he climaxed. He lay silently for another minute, then climbed off the table, grabbed his clothes, and scurried to the bathroom to change. I tidied up a bit in the glow of that one candle. I put on my gym shorts and waited by the massage table.

Coming out of the bathroom dressed and ready to go, Art had my money, two hundred dollars, in hand. I took it from him and said thank you, but you could tell he was not happy to be leaving. He acted like he wanted to kiss me and stay with me the rest of the afternoon.

"Call me again when you're in Denver," I whispered and kissed him on the cheek.

Art gave me a bear hug. "Thank you, Mike," he said with a lot of sadness in his voice.

He rubbed my shoulders, opened the door, and left. Once I heard him get in the elevator, I turned on the overhead lights in the apartment and got the room ready for my next client, who would be arriving in a few hours.

I checked the room to make sure he didn't leave anything behind. I've had client leave watches, cell phones, even wedding rings behind. Art was always good about picking up after himself.

Art from Kansas City.

That's how the man I later discovered to be Ted Haggard, the founder of New Life Church and the president of the 30-million-member National Association of Evangelicals, first introduced himself.

I would love to tell you that from the day we met in June 2003 I remember him as being unique or odd. He had some quirks, such as an incredible shyness, but so did many of my clients. And there was nothing about him physically that made you take notice.

Except for his smile. His grin was big and sincere, almost goofy. You couldn't miss it. Even when he was sad, like when our sessions came to an end, he still managed to muster a smile that brightened the room. Art, or Ted, always seemed to be in a good mood. He was never bitchy or mean.

He came to every appointment very well groomed and dressed. His nails were always trimmed and his hair perfect. He was always clean-shaven, and he kept his body clean as well. Believe me, that's a big plus in my business.

Business casual is how I would describe his dress. He never wore shorts or just a T-shirt. He always wore a nice shirt with a collar, looking like the tie had come off just a few minutes earlier. He always wore jeans and never wore dress slacks. All the way around, he always looked great, just like all the guys in those Levi's commercials on television. When we first met, I knew he wasn't openly gay, but I remember thinking that he sure did dress like a preppy gay boy.

There was shame in his eyes, but Art never wore a hat or sunglasses or tried to disguise himself. I could tell he wasn't proud of his visits to me, but that didn't bother him enough to stay away or hide his face.

He was attractive but not in an obvious way. Perhaps the best way to describe his appeal is to call it subtle. He was just one of the guys—a guy who had needs, and my job was to help him meet those needs. Art was basically no different than most of my other clients. He had an average build and average looks. He wasn't fat, but he wasn't muscular. He was average below the waist as well. He was just an average, pleasant guy.

When he first called me, it was a typical bright sunny morning in Denver. I had just returned home after playing tennis. Shortly after breakfast, my phone rang; the caller ID read "unavailable."

"Hi, this is Mike," I answered.

"Hi, Mike, my name is Art from Kansas City," said the light and happy voice on the other end. For more than a year, he never said, "This is Art." He always said, "This is Art *from Kansas City*." To this day, I can only guess that he said that because he didn't want me to know he was from Colorado Springs. The two big industries there are Christianity and defense. Perhaps he feared I would stereotype him as wearing either a vestment or a uniform. Not surprisingly, almost all my clients from the Springs were, in fact, either clergy or military. And they were some of my best customers.

"I saw your ad for escorting," he continued. At the time, I had ads on several Web sites, and one of my ads appeared in the escorting section. "I'm visiting Denver and would like to schedule an appointment with you."

So far so good, I thought. He didn't ask if I was a hooker or a hustler, or if I'd take it up the ass. I'd always hang up on guys who asked that. It's an issue of respect. If they can't respect me, I have no business doing business with them. "What day would you like?"

"How about Tuesday at two o'clock?"

I took a quick look at my pocket calendar. I used a small paper calendar where I'd scribble down appointments for massage or weight training. I'd never write down any of my escorting appointments. When someone asked for a specific day and time, I'd check the calendar only to make sure I had not booked something else. I always remembered when and where my escort appointments were.

"Tuesday at two will be fine," I confirmed. I gave him my address and explained how to get there. With new clients, I also state my rate: "It starts at two hundred dollars."

Art from Kansas City confirmed that he was fine with everything. Like in any business, if you don't discuss price from the beginning, the situation can snowball later. That was one of my many business practices that kept my losses to a minimum.

Prior to Art arriving, I got the massage room ready. When he first came to see me, I was living on Sherman Street near downtown Denver. I rented a studio unit next door to my condo, and that's where I entertained both escorting and massage clients. The massage table, which stood just three feet off the ground, was right in the middle of the minimally furnished room. I put black construction paper on the windows so no light could come in. For those who wanted even more privacy, I had blinds and drapes I could shut. There was a small dresser where I kept fresh towels and other supplies, like massage lotion. I had a futon and television just in case a client wanted to watch some porn.

When I greeted clients, I usually wore just a pair of gym shorts and nothing else, and that's what I wore for Art.

He buzzed my unit at two o'clock on the nose. "It's Art from Kansas City."

"C'mon in." I buzzed him in and stood in the hallway so he could see me when he got off the elevator.

Art stepped from the elevator wearing a pair of jeans and a polo shirt. I got the sense that he wanted to make a good first impression. He smiled wide, but as he approached my massage room his smile turned down a bit. His eyes avoided mine.

"Nice to meet you, Art." Since he was a new client, I needed to get a sense of what he wanted. I wanted to encourage trust between us, so I started by asking him some fairly innocuous questions like "How are you?" and "Enjoying your visit?"

Art wasn't dismissive, but it was obvious he did not want to talk. His eyes kept looking at everything but my face. He was nervous, but something told me that he'd been to an escort before. After years in the business, I was very good at reading faces, especially right before a sexual encounter. My sense was that Art was dealing with a lot of shame or guilt.

"Can I use the bathroom?" he asked.

I gestured to the bathroom door, which was right next to the front door. "Use whatever you want in there," I offered. On the counter, I kept many basic men's grooming items, like deodorant, hair gel, hair spray, lotion, combs, and cologne.

Art came out of the bathroom still fully clothed. "Can you make the room any darker?" he asked. I knew he was nervous, so I wasn't offended by anything he said.

I went to the window and shut the drapes. Five candles were placed throughout the room, so I went over to a candle by the window and blew it out. He did not say anything, so I went to another candle and blew it out as well. He was still quiet, so I went across the room to another candle and blew that one out.

"Darker, please," he asked when just two candles shone. I went to another candle in a corner of the room and blew it out, then took the last remaining candle out of its holder to dull its brightness a bit. I placed it on the stand by itself.

"Perfect!" The place was dark, but there was enough light to move about. It was darkness that Art needed before he could disrobe. Many of my clients got naked right away and didn't care much about lighting, especially since I was on the third floor and no one could look in. At first, I thought maybe Art wanted it so dark because he had a deformity that he didn't want me to see.

I stood behind the kitchen curtain to give him some privacy. I watched as he hung up his shirt and jeans and put the rest of his clothes on a chair, then climbed on the massage table and lay face down. I did not tell him to do that, so that, too, told me he had done this before. Men who hire escorts often start a session with some type of massage, which somehow makes everything they are doing legitimate.

Walking over to the table with supplies, I put heated massage lotion on my hands. I then stood at the head of the massage table and reached over Art to massage his lower back, putting my crotch right into his head. His face, nestled in the cradle, did not move, even after I started pushing my groin into his skull.

"That feels good," he said. A moment later, he brought his arms forward to play with my ass. "You've got a nice ass," he told me.

Depending on the client, I may or may not respond. With Art, I sensed he needed to make a connection, so I whispered,

"Thank you." I continued to rub him down for another ten or so minutes. His hands were fondling me all over, though he never got comfortable enough to put his face into my crotch.

It was so dark in the room that I couldn't tell if Art had any distinguishing features. Just by touching him, I could tell he wasn't flabby, muscular, overly hairy, or smooth skinned. He seemed to have a nondescript kind of body, and from my end of the transaction that was preferable.

When I told him to turn over, he did.

As I stood beside him, he began rubbing my chest. "I really like how you trim yourself," he said of my trimmed chest hair. "I like that a lot."

Art didn't ask me any questions of a sexual nature that first day. He was enjoying the experience as best he could.

"Do you want release?" I asked him.

He said yes, so I spent a few minutes stroking him. I could tell it had been awhile since he had done that. It was over and done with in less than two minutes.

Once we were done, though, I could almost see the shame come over him. I placed a dry hand towel on his groin, and he snatched it up quickly. Some guys lie there for awhile and enjoy the afterglow, but not Art. He got up quickly, as though his mother had caught him naked with another boy.

"You can take a shower if you like."

"No, thank you," he said dully.

I slipped on my gym shorts and tidied the room while I waited for him to come out of the bathroom.

Stepping out dressed and ready to go, he handed me two hundred dollars in twenties, saying just "Thank you." Before I could say anything, he opened the front door and let himself out. It was as though he had just done something that he'd rather forget.

Perhaps what stood out most about Art was that nothing about him stood out. He wasn't pushy or obnoxious. He didn't draw attention to himself. Most importantly, he paid me what he owed me and didn't try to jack with me on price. He was just a nice, quiet guy who treated me with respect.

For all those reasons, I was hoping I would see him again. It was clear that he was dealing with a lot of issues. Perhaps we could deal with them in the future.

Escorting is a thankless job.

You are providing a service that has value only in the moment. It's an important service, no doubt, but your clients rarely praise you the way they might praise a doctor, a waitress, or even a plumber. The only way you know for sure that you are doing a good job is when your clients keep coming back.

When I would first meet a client like Art, I never tried to guess whether or not they would come back. Sometimes they didn't come back because you truly were not what they wanted, and I understood that. Often, the cost of my services put me out of the reach of most men, but I would never offer a free visit or discount. There was never any need to do that. I also would not give referrals to other escorts. I did not know any other escort well enough, and even if I did, why would I want to give business away?

About a month after his first visit, I received another blocked call. "Hi, Mike, it's Art from Kansas City," he said.

"How are you, Art?"

"Would you have an appointment available around three this afternoon?"

I looked at my calendar and saw nothing booked, so I said sure. Generally, I charged more than two hundred dollars if clients called on such short notice, but if I had nothing planned and was available—and especially if I needed the money—I would see someone on the spot for no extra charge, unless it was late at night.

Being an escort is like being a bartender. I may not always remember someone's name, but I always remember what they like. After just one visit, I remembered what Art liked and how he liked it. The beauty of his tastes was that they were so simple.

"Hi, Mike, it's Art from Kansas City." I swear, he said that every time.

I buzzed him in and waited in the hallway, just in case he forgot where to go. Walking in, he seemed impressed that I had the room set up exactly the same way as last time, with the curtains drawn and just one tea candle outside its holder on a small table. "You remembered," he said with clenched joy. And then off he scurried into the bathroom.

I got naked and waited out of view. As quickly as he could, Art got undressed, hung up his clothes, and lay face down on the massage table. I emerged from the kitchen, squirted some freshly heated massage lotion onto my hands, and began rubbing down his back as I stood with my crotch in his face. As I rubbed his back, Art began playing with my ass more aggressively than before.

If it's all starting to sound routine, you've discovered the key to making a man happy. Most men don't deal well with change. They want things to be a certain way and see no need to change it unless they are forced to. By first figuring out the script, sticking to it, and offering it again time after time, I ensured that my clients kept coming back.

I felt Art might like to try some light role-playing. "You like my tight ass?" I said in a guttural, sexy tone. I was trying to see how he responded to dirty talk.

"Oh, yeah!" he exclaimed.

So far so good. I let him play with my ass while I spoke dirty to him. What I said wasn't too nasty, just a bit more suggestive than normal. "Do you like my rock-hard body and my big balls?" I asked aggressively.

"It's hot!"

Within minutes, he flipped himself over and was clearly aroused. In fact, he was close to releasing, so I played with him until he climaxed. Like most men, he was done within a matter of minutes.

And once again, after he was done, he barely paused to regain his breath before he sat up, hopped off the massage table, grabbed his clothes, and scurried to the bathroom. Seeing this pattern emerge, I felt bad for him. I could see he had issues but had no clue as to what they were. The upside for me was that I didn't have to work very hard for him. His needs were minimal, and I met them simply by being in his presence. Whatever was going on in his life would not let him enjoy himself.

Art never called me on weekends and only once called for a night appointment. During the three years I saw him, he scheduled appointments between one and four in the afternoon on weekdays. Many clients who were clergymen would schedule afternoon appointments. One used to come see me after he was done visiting the sick in hospitals or nursing homes. Men of the cloth almost never saw me on weekends because they were usually working.

Fall was approaching, and the leaves on Colorado's aspen trees were turning golden. Within thirty days of our last session, Art from Kansas City called me again from an untraceable number. He again requested a weekday afternoon slot, and again, it was the same routine: one tea candle, undressing in the dark, putting his hands on my butt and his face in my crotch. He'd flip over, and I'd help him release. And once he was finished, he'd scurry to the bathroom, put his clothes back on, and leave as quietly as possible.

In my job—and trust me, it's a job—I had to be part entertainer and part psychologist. My customers often unloaded on me because they had nowhere else to turn. I listened and did the best I could for them. Art never unloaded on me, at least not during the first year, but I could tell that he wanted to talk. It was almost as if he wanted to be my buddy. He enjoyed being touched and the sex, to be sure, but he wanted more of a bond.

As the months progressed, he started to lighten up a bit. He started asking me questions, all tame, and I would share my knowledge of gay sex or whatever the topic happened to be.

One time he wanted some grooming advice.

"Do you use clippers or a razor blade?"

I told him I used a razor blade on my groin and clippers on the rest of my body. Then I put my hands on his pubic area to show him where and how to trim himself. He enjoyed the manual stimulation, and I'm sure he appreciated the grooming advice, too.

After about five months, he tried performing oral sex on me. He was very timid about it, so I let him take as long as he needed. When it comes to sex with another man, there is always an element of surprise, no matter how slow you take it or how timid you are.

More often than not, nothing much happens physically between two guys other than the fact that they are both naked and one or both reaches climax. What often does happen, however, is intimacy, and that scares a lot of people. It's one thing for guys to have a sex drive, but when men start sharing feelings, that creates all kinds of discomfort for a lot of people. I understand, because that's how society is, but intimacy was usually at the core of what I did as an escort.

What I provided for men like Art had little to do with sex. These men want intimacy with another man, something they're unable to experience elsewhere. Sure, there were some kinky fantasies that I fulfilled. Men like Art, however, just want to be held or touched. I'm not making this up. What I provided was different than the raw sex you get from a hustler or hooker. If you want an analogy, what I provided was more along the lines of a combat nurse.

I have seen literally hundreds of wounded men like Art, all showing the emotional battle scars of trying to live a life other than the one they want to live. These men would come to me depressed, needy, and usually with little or no self-respect. Sometimes they were in situations that they could not get out of, a kind of war zone. I would bring a wounded troop into my care, and it was my job, if possible, to mend and patch them up. Then, once they were stable enough to leave my care, I would send them back into combat. It's not a stretch, really. These men wouldn't be coming to me if everything were fine and honest in their lives. Art certainly was not seeing me because his life was going well. I knew that from the moment I met him.

During another visit around Christmas, Art asked me to lie on top of him. That was a big step for him, one that told me he wanted to get more physical. The massage table was sturdy and could hold up to six hundred pounds. Art lay on his back, and I climbed on top of him, pressing my genitals against his. Once Art was comfortable with me on top, he put his arms around me and held me.

Even though my legs were getting tired, Art was enjoying

the mere physical contact of our bodies. But come the end of the hour, once things were over, they were over for Art. That first year, without fail, he always got up quickly from the massage table, grabbed his clothes, and raced to the bathroom. Once the bathroom door opened, he would pay me, say thank you, and leave.

Once I saw tears form in his eyes, but I didn't say anything. When a man cries in front of another man, especially one he does not know well, there is some deep-seated pain there. I felt bad for him. I would have loved to ask him what was going on, but he didn't want to go there. He wanted as few words as possible, and that was okay. He was getting something from our visits, I hoped. Over the course of a year, I had become a monthly expense, just like his gasoline or his cable bill.

One time, he placed his wedding ring on top of his underwear on the chair. The light from the candle reflected off of it. I began to wonder why he didn't take the time to put the ring in a pocket or hide it somehow, as he usually would have. I estimate that almost 80 percent of my clients were married men. Art was trying to tell me one of two things: *I'm happily married so don't even think about falling in love with me*, or, *I'm married and miserable so tell me everyone else is miserable, too.* At the end of the hour when he picked up his clothes, I watched as he put his ring back on. My only concern was that it looked like a very expensive ring, and I didn't want him to lose it.

In 2004, Art totally surprised me one time by greeting me with a big kiss. Many of my clients who weren't comfortable being gay would avoid kissing another man, because they thought it was a sign that you really are a homo. Art's kiss came out of left field. I wanted to be careful not to discourage him, but I also had to let him know that I wasn't really into kissing clients. Even though I charged a lot per session, I would let clients know that I was still in charge.

I turned my lips from Art and let him kiss me on the cheek. He hesitated a bit but seemed not to be troubled by my response. I wanted him to take his time, and I tried, while saying little, to let him know that everything would be all right. But rather than let the moment slide, I pushed him toward the massage table and prompted him to get undressed.

One time, in February or March of 2004, when he called me to make an appointment, my caller ID showed a 719 area code, which meant he was calling from Colorado Springs.

"Mike, I'm flying into Denver later today. Can I see you when I get there?"

Well, either he was flying from Colorado Springs to Denver or he was lying, but who cared?

"I'd really like to see you tonight!" he said.

I looked down at my watch.

"You'd be on my way home," Art said. "I'd really like to see you."

I rubbed my eyes, blinked a few times, and then said sure.

"Thank you, Mike." And then, click, and all was quiet again.

When I saw him that night, I wore a jockstrap instead of gym shorts, just to vary things a bit. He seemed to really like it and asked if he could try it on. I let him wear it, and over the course of the next few visits, I let him try on some other underwear, including a couple of off-the-shelf thongs. He seemed to especially like the Stars-and-Stripes thong, which I had received as a gag gift a few years earlier.

Another time during that first year, he asked, "Can we just sit on the couch?" I said sure and took him over to the futon, where we both sat and rubbed each other for awhile. The room was again lit with just one tea candle, but Art remained clothed, refusing to undress until he was ready to get on the massage table. He showed a desire to become more intimate.

If I could think of one word to describe Art during that first year, it would be *gentleman*, because Art truly was a gentle man. He would never try anything rough or sneaky with me. He never challenged me or tried anything fast. More than anything else, he seemed to want my affection. He never said he loved me, and that was good. But I could tell he was feeling something.

He could not get enough of me. Given the choice, I believe he would have spent much more time with me. There was always eagerness when he called to book an appointment and incredible sadness each time he left. It hurt me to know that when our hour was up, he had to go back to the life that he had made for himself. I had no idea what that life was, but I could tell he did not enjoy it as much as he enjoyed seeing me.

Many first-year clients get nervous, and some probably have a drink or smoke pot to help them lighten up before they arrive. Art, however, would only drink water. As someone who is into bodybuilding, I found that healthy, and again, I tried to encourage him whenever I could.

I had many clients who fell in love with me and showered me with roses, champagne, coffee table books of nude males, and gift certificates to local restaurants. It all meant nothing to me. Some clients even wanted to take me to Europe to play out some exotic fantasy they had. I wished they could see our relationship as just business, and thankfully, Art came off as understanding that, at least during that first year. He was not interested in a relationship.

Art's life seemed so fragmented, each part disconnected from the other parts. My job wasn't to help him sort it all out.

I was being paid to be just one piece of the puzzle. I was like a toy he played with when he wanted to and put away when he had to.

If only all my clients had been that easy to decipher. The truth is there were many who touched me more deeply than Art ever did.

One was a man who was visiting from Italy and wanted to book an appointment several days ahead. He was very specific, requesting the two o'clock time slot on Friday afternoon. Leading up to our meeting, he called every day to confirm our appointment. I assured him everything was set, figuring he was calling a lot either because he was very nervous or very married. When Friday rolled around, he called again around noon to verify, and this time he used a phrase I heard all too often: "Hey, can I ask you something?"

When a client says that, get ready for a request that may push the envelope of good taste and judgment.

"Would it be okay if I wore women's lingerie to my appointment?"

Oh, is that all? "Sure," I replied. I never personally got into ladies' lingerie or related articles, but if it made clients feel comfortable, then why not?

When two o'clock rolled around, I stepped out on my balcony, which overlooked the street, looking for a guy to show up in drag. I saw a handsome guy dressed in nice jeans and a collared shirt get out of a truck and walk toward my building.

A moment later, my phone rang. "It's Giovanni."

"C'mon up," I said, buzzing him in. He knocked on my door, and there stood the man from the street. I was pleasantly surprised to see this handsome Italian man standing at my door. I welcomed him into my apartment, took him to the massage room, lit a few candles, and fluffed some pillows as he undressed. He lay down on the massage table wearing nothing but a pair of lacy women's panties.

As I put massage lotion on my hands, I could tell that he wanted to talk, but he was nervous. So, as I did with any client who was a bit uneasy, I smiled, touched him gently, and tried to make him feel more at home. Soon his panties came off, a light conversation started, and his tension seemed to melt away. I could tell clients were relaxing when they appeared to sink more deeply into the massage table. That always made me feel good—helping someone relax and enjoy the hour. He wasn't chatty, but he did have a lot to share.

Yet as our session wound down, Giovanni's sadness was obvious. That's common—feeling sad as the fantasy hour winds down to yield to reality. Giovanni got off the table, packed up his things in his backpack, and put his boy clothes back on, all without saying a word. He handed me the money, but I could see in his eyes that he was feeling a bit empty. I said thank you, gave him a big bear hug, and watched him leave.

Later that night, I received another call from him.

"Can I book another appointment for tomorrow?" he asked.

I took a quick look at my calendar. "Yes, Giovanni, that will work fine."

"Can I come at two o'clock again?"

I said yes, wished him a good evening, and went to bed.

Like clockwork, he buzzed my apartment at two o'clock sharp, carrying the same backpack. Inside the massage room, he was wearing women's undergarments that were much more elaborate, much more frilly, all made of beautiful red silk. I could tell he was more at ease with me this time, telling me a whole lot more about his life in France and Italy.

"I want you to know how comfortable I felt with you yesterday," he said with a slight but sexy European accent. I said I considered it an honor that he wanted to see me two days in a row. I wasn't lying about that.

Yet once again, as our time came to a close, I could see the sadness in his eyes as he gathered his things, gave me the money, hugged me, kissed me on the cheek, and left—all without saying a word. I felt bad for him. Maybe this was all he could do to explore his hidden feelings, what some people might call his feminine side.

To my surprise, he called later that night, asking if he could come over a third day in a row. I booked him for two o'clock.

Just three visits in, and we were already into a routine. He enjoyed touching me, but that was not the main reason he paid two hundred dollars a pop to see me. He enjoyed women's clothes. For some reason, this was the only outlet he had for dressing as he pleased and being with whom he wanted.

For his next appointment, Giovanni took off his clothes to reveal new lingerie and a garter belt with nylons. "You look great," I told him, and he was flattered by my comment. We did our usual touch and fondle, but as things progressed, tears welled up in his eyes.

"What's wrong?" I asked carefully.

"Mike, I cannot tell you how much this means to me," he confessed, wiping his eyes with a tissue I handed him. "This is such a dark secret I live with and do not share with any of my friends or acquaintances."

Boy, do I know about secrets! Giovanni grabbed my hand and held it. "You have made me feel special and accepted." He started crying.

It was close to the end of our session, so I lifted him off the table and gave him a great big hug. "Everything is going to be okay," I whispered. "I want you to feel comfortable with me, so just be yourself." I thought about extending the session for no charge, but I decided against it, trying to be as businesslike as possible. He again gathered his things, kissed me, and left.

It came as no surprise when I got another call from him later that night, asking if he could come over yet again the following day. He said he didn't want to get naked or have sex, just enjoy my company.

"I would be honored," I told him.

When he arrived the next day at, yes, two o'clock, he had a gift bag for me. In it were gourmet wines, chocolates, and sauces, all things he said he enjoyed from Europe. He said that he hoped I would enjoy them as much as he did. I thanked him as we sat on the couch, hugging and touching each other without doing anything sexual.

He told me this would be the last time he could see me before he left the United States.

"Please be at peace with yourself," I told him. "And screw everyone else!"

He cried as he was leaving, and hell, I almost started to cry. *All this man wants to do is dress in the clothes that he likes and that turn him on, and look at all the heartache it's causing him.* Ironically, that charade and its pain is one of the main reasons I was in business. Intimacy among men is so rare that when they find a place where they can get it, many men will do or pay anything. Clients like Giovanni and Art are just two names among many.

So, you see, a good escort not only has sex but also provides joy to people who may not have much otherwise.

I received a call from an acquaintance. He told me that he and his partner had taken in a friend, a man named Paul, who was just fifty but in the advanced stages of Alzheimer's disease. My friend wanted to provide Paul with a massage and some man-to-man contact.

We scheduled an appointment for the next day at noon. When he arrived, Paul handed me a piece of paper with a name and phone number to call when our appointment was over. I had not been around anyone who was so disabled that they needed my help to make a phone call. I was honored to help him, but I was also a bit nervous.

Paul was a very gentle man with a very round face, a big smile, and a very happy disposition, given his circumstances. I took Paul to the massage table and helped him lay facedown. I was trying extra hard to make him feel comfortable. I remember how he wanted to talk the entire time I was touching him.

As I touched him, Paul told me how he had quit his job in aviation due to his illness. Unable to live independently, he'd sold his house and all of his belongings. He also told me that the younger you are when you develop Alzheimer's, the faster it progresses.

"You've got some great friends," I told him. "Don't worry, they'll take care of you." As I rubbed him down, he was smiling as best he could. I was trying not to cry.

The whole time, Paul never cried or displayed any sadness. In fact, he would occasionally make a joke, and we would both laugh. It was difficult for him, but we would laugh anyway.

Paul had been openly gay most of his adult life, so he wasn't trying to hide anything by coming to me. He was simply finding the intimacy that he had not been able to get since he became ill.

When our session was over, I called the number on the paper. I then walked him downstairs to a waiting car.

I saw him once a month for a total of six visits. With each visit, he was visibly worse. At our last few appointments, he could not remember where the massage room or the bathroom was. On his last visit, he forgot to take off his clothes. By nature, I am a very patient person, and I was determined to make his visits as enjoyable, memorable, and erotic as possible. After that, I never saw him again.

CHAPTER 2

HOW I BECAME AN ESCORT

□

"How did you get into this business?" Art asked.

He was all dressed and ready to go, but for some reason, he wasn't in a hurry to leave. I hadn't checked the clock to see if we had gone past an hour.

"I wish I could tell you how I got started," I told him. "It just kinda happened."

Art smiled and rubbed my chest, which he loved to do. "Tell me about some of your more interesting clients."

Normally, I felt rushed and liked to get clients in and out the door. That spring afternoon in 2004, however, I felt relaxed. "Can I get you a bottle of water?" I offered.

Art's face lit up. "That would be nice," he replied. I took him by the hand and sat him down at my dining room table.

"Would you like to hear the raunchy stories or the touching ones?"

"You have some touching stories?" he asked, apparently surprised that there might be some compassion involved in escorting.

"You'd be surprised at how many clients are just average Joes who need to be touched."

I was just eighteen when I was offered money for sex for the first time. Fresh out of high school, I was ready to explore the world, especially the world of man-on-man sex. I knew about

35

certain parks where men hung out, but since there was also a handful of gay bars in Denver, I figured I'd start there. Like many young adults, I had a fake ID and used it to get into the bars where I might find older men, the kind I've always found most attractive.

In 1975, the gay world was still underground in Denver. Most nightclubs had back-alley entrances and no windows. A popular wall color back then was black. I didn't understand all the secrecy, but I accepted it as a normal part of gay culture. I really didn't know any better.

I was in a neighborhood gay bar for about an hour, just hanging out drinking a beer. I was by myself, hoping to get picked up. I'd never tried anal sex, and I had a passing curiosity about rougher kinds of sex. I was hoping an older man, a "daddy," would take me to his place and show me the ropes.

A man in his forties came up to me and started talking to me. He offered to buy me a drink, and I accepted. We made some small talk as Led Zeppelin played on the jukebox.

"See my friend over there?" he asked. "He'd like to spend some time with you." Taking another sip of his highball, he added, "He can pay you for your time."

I wasn't sure what to make of the offer. I went to the bar just to have sex. Why was this man suddenly offering me money?

I thought about saying no, but then I asked, "How much?" I was more curious about the offer than put off by it. I wasn't offended because, honestly, I needed the money. It just seemed odd that without even knowing me, someone would open his wallet.

"I'm sure he'll make it worth your time," the man replied.

Perhaps I should have been scared by that response, but I wasn't. I was young and horny and willing to have sex with anyone who asked. His friend was a decent-looking man. I didn't have to be anywhere. I was just a boy from a small Denver suburb. "Why not?" I told him.

I went to the other side of the bar and met the man. He would not have been my first choice, but I hadn't been approached by anyone else. We exchanged a few pleasantries, and the next thing I knew, we were leaving the bar and walking to his apartment a few blocks away. As soon as we got in the door, clothes started falling to the ground.

Sex between two men can take a variety of forms. Sometimes there's anal intercourse, but often it's just rubbing and touching, and maybe a little oral sex and then ejaculation. It's often quick, sometimes lasting no more than five minutes.

I spent about two hours with this man, fondling, rubbing, and holding him. For an eighteen-year-old, it was quite exciting. I'd had sex with boys my own age in high school and had even had sex with a teacher, but I had never spent an afternoon making love like that.

When it was all over, I put on my clothes, and he put a wad of cash in my pocket. I thanked him and kissed him again as I left, leaving him naked on his couch. Walking back to the bar where my car was parked, I counted the various bills. There were ten bills, and each one was a twenty.

Holy shit! Two hundred dollars. I could buy a car with that kind of money.

I was flipping out, in a good way. I couldn't believe that someone would actually pay me to do what I wanted to do anyway. It was a mindblower. I decided not to go back to the bar. I drove home, stopping on the way to eat at a semi-nice restaurant, hoping my mother wouldn't ask me how my day had gone.

That night as I looked over some college catalogs, I wondered if perhaps I could do it again. Could I again get a man to pay me for sex? The concept was new to me, to be sure. I knew what prostitution was, but I thought that applied only to women. This was different, but I wasn't sure how. Maybe these men were paying me to have sex because it was so taboo to even say you had sexual feelings for another man. This was their way of keeping everything quiet.

I wasn't sure what to think. I wanted to go to college, but I would need money. Plus, I wanted more sex. Call me naïve, but I figured I'd go back to the bar sometime soon to see if I could get picked up again.

The next time was just as surprising to me as the first. I was sitting alone in a gay bar called David's when yet another man approached me.

"See my friend over there?" the man said, pointing to a large, Hispanic man who wasn't all that attractive. "He'd really like to meet you." The large man cracked a smile and waved. Without saying a word, I smiled and stared at my drink. I couldn't believe this was happening again.

"How much do you charge?" the man asked me.

I gave him a curious look, not sure how to respond. I was acting cool, but I had no idea what I was doing. Before I could say anything, the man added, "He owns a couple of popular restaurants, so he has money." The man kept looking me over. "Nice arms, by the way."

I put down my glass. "It starts at two hundred dollars," I told him. Honestly, I have no idea where those words came from. I probably said two hundred dollars because that's what I'd gotten last time. That price would probably scare him off, but if it didn't, I was that much richer.

"Let's go meet him," the man said.

I was a bit panicked and was hoping he would just walk away. I got off my stool and walked over to meet my "client." That night was the first time I remember taking the trouble to observe everything around me, a habit I still have to this day. Mind you, I had no idea what I was doing. I relied on the only thing I had, which was my gut.

I shook hands with the large Hispanic man and talked with him for a bit. How are you? Aren't we having nice weather? Yes, the price of gasoline is ridiculous. Then, to my surprise, my client said he just wanted a blow job in the men's room. I was more than a little nervous about that. Men got arrested all the time for having sex in public restrooms. Nonetheless, I followed him into the bathroom. Even though David's was a bit more private than the toilets at, say, a truck stop, I still worried about the police. It was a dark restroom with black walls, and I knew I was not the only man to give a blow job in there that night. We waited until a man washing his hands left, then we walked into the same stall. Within seconds, he had unzipped his pants and I was on my knees. I was lucky that the guy was clean and not aggressive.

After about ten minutes, my client was done and zipped up his pants. Right in the stall he handed me two hundred-dollar bills. When we opened the stall door, we saw another man was standing by the sink. Far from being offended, he had an inviting look, as if to say he was ready to do me next.

I went back to my corner of the bar and sat with another beer. Nothing happened the rest of the night, but it didn't matter to me. Something was going on, and I wasn't sure what to make of it. Maybe this was how sex between younger and older men happened.

It seemed that every time I went out after that, I would get offers of cash for sex, even on weeknights. Even on nights when I was ready to burst with semen and was willing to give it away, I was offered money. I had no one to talk to about it, so I just accepted the fact that men wanted to pay me for my time.

I've always known how to talk to people and make them feel comfortable. I was never just a bunch of muscles with no personality. I always interacted well with my clients, no matter what their background or hang-ups were. But to be honest, my body was my biggest draw. The first thing people notice about me is my biceps and my chest. I can thank my brother Russ for that.

Russ was quite the boy, much more so than I was. He was big. Not fat, but stocky and muscular, and it served him well back in the 1950s and 1960s. As a teenager, he excelled in baseball and football and anything athletic.

There was a lot of pressure on me to be like him. Even though I didn't understand what was going on within me, I knew I was different, and my older brother knew I was different, too.

I don't know what it was that caused it, and I've tried not to speculate, but he had an incredibly bad temper. The slightest thing would set him off. I remember how, more than once, he would be so angry that he would punch holes through the walls in our house. He also tried to punch holes in me.

I was a scrawny kid. There was nothing that stood out about me. I had a caring heart, but I had no particular talent in athletics or anything else. I was content to spend time with my mother, or my grandmother, or my great-grandmother, whom I called Nanny. If I couldn't be with one of these women, then I wanted to be left alone. But with Russ in the house, that wasn't going to happen.

Besides being very good at sports, my brother also had

charisma. He always had several girlfriends, and as best I could tell, he was a favorite of the popular crowd at school.

It seemed that every chance he got, Russ took pleasure in calling me names and taking swings at me. He used his superior size and strength to get his way with me, which was ironic since I would have let him do whatever he wanted. All he had to do was ask.

When Mom and Dad would go out for the night, they would leave Russ and me at home alone, and I would be filled with terror. Russ knew how to throw punches when parents or teachers weren't looking, so when we were alone, we could never sit in front of the TV or listen to records together. Once Mom and Dad left the house, I would have to barricade myself in my room for the entire evening.

Some of my most severe beatings happened when Russ's friends came over. Maybe he saw it as some sort of show. Russ seemed to take joy in beating the crap out of me while his friends watched. I don't remember once hearing any of his friends telling him to stop.

My parents assumed it was just horseplay between brothers. They would yell, "Stop fighting, boys!" and somehow that was supposed to make things better. I was never good at standing up for myself. I always wanted to be the peacemaker who brought joy to the world, but at a very early age I discovered there was a downside to being nice.

Russ beat up a lot of other kids, not just me. When I got to high school, I found out how bad his reputation was. He used to beat up guys for no reason at all, and when you do that, people become suspicious of your whole family. I certainly had no interest in beating up anyone, but going into high school with his legacy preceding me was tough.

Back then, comic books and advertisers talked all the time

about the ninety-eight-pound weakling who couldn't defend himself. The solution was to start lifting weights and build muscle and become "a man." Knowing there was a weight-lifting class at my junior high school, I figured I'd give it a try.

I can only imagine what the weight-lifting coaches thought of me when I first approached them. I clearly did not have a muscular build. I would like to think that I won them over with my spirit and my attitude. The truth was that I was stronger than I looked.

I was about thirteen when I first lay on a bench and attempted to bench press. From the first day, the gym teachers were impressed. I was a natural. Without any instruction, my form was good and my strength, especially for a preteen, amazed them. All the gym instructors noticed my ability. That led to more personal attention from them, and I ate it up. I'd never had personal attention or tutoring in any subject before.

I dove into the sport. I bought every muscle magazine I could, and when I had saved up enough money, I bought supplements like protein powder and tablets of amino acids. This was a big change for me. I was used to being afraid all the time because of my older brother. I was used to hating myself. I considered myself ugly, and I certainly wasn't popular. Weight lifting gave me a chance to stand out. It worked for me for two important reasons: I was good at it, and I could do it alone. I didn't have to be a team player, and I didn't have to have friends to do it well.

By the time I entered high school, I had developed enough muscle and skill to compete in power-lifting competitions. I weighed about 165 pounds in 1973, when I entered my junior year. I could bench press two hundred pounds, do a squat with five hundred pounds, and a dead lift with six hundred pounds. For a sixteen-year-old, that was considered excellent.

I was taking first place in my division at almost every meet I competed in, and I was feeling great. For the first time in my life, I felt like a winner. Even though I was still shy and pimply, I was gaining self-confidence. I was even being noticed by fellow classmates, who had simply ignored me in the past.

Everything was going great. Only one thing was missing. My parents never came to my meets. Unlike other boys, I had no family member in the bleachers enjoying my achievements. Oh, sure, when I brought the trophies home, I heard nothing but congratulations and praise, but it was only after the fact. I think my parents did not understand that weight lifting was a sport, just like baseball and football. I probably won twenty or more weight lifting trophies, but mine got buried among all the trophies Russ had won for other sports.

Even so, my place in the world did start to change once my muscles developed. To meet the personal bodybuilding goals I set for myself at such a young age took a lot of hard and dangerous work. When I competed, I would start by trying to bulk up to 190 pounds and then put myself on a very strict diet high in protein and low in carbohydrates. Then I'd cut back significantly on my food intake while at the same time increasing my cardio workouts. If I started training with 12 percent body fat, my goal would be to get down to about 5 or 6 percent body fat. I did that by basically starving myself. But given the response I was getting, I saw no reason to stop.

Years later, I saw the willingness of older men to pay me for sex as the payoff for that effort. I admit I was flattered by all the attention. Normally, men would say something like "God, you've got a hot body" and then start rubbing my arms or my chest. My face wasn't bad either, but my muscles seemed to be my biggest attraction.

Until I took off my pants.

When I was fooling around with other boys as a kid, it was obvious that I was better endowed than most guys. As an adult, I always made sure to wear shorts or pants that showed off my assets. Due to all the weight lifting and exercise, I also developed a nice butt.

But as I turned twenty, I still wasn't sure what I was doing. I was getting paid for sex, that much I knew. It seemed like all I had to do was walk into a bar, and within a short time, someone would approach me with an offer of money. I had no idea if this was normal or not. In the 1970s, homosexuality wasn't talked about much, so how could I know what was normal? Someone back then called me an escort, and that term seemed to stick, though I had no idea why. I was savvy enough to stay out of trouble, but I wasn't smart enough to figure out what I was doing. If I had been, I might have done something different.

For all the success I had selling myself, my ability to make and keep friends was lagging. I didn't develop friendships with the people I got together with sexually. I was barely nineteen when I stopped taking off my pants unless someone was paying me. I wanted to draw a clear line between business and pleasure. Then, in my early twenties, I became friends with two clients.

One was a nice-looking man in his late fifties named Alan who'd been one of my very first clients. He was about six-foot two with a slender build and was just coming out. He was a professor and a divorced father of two.

One of my haunts was this gay country-western bar. After the success I had with my first few escorting ventures, I figured that if I put a little effort into it, I might attract more and better clients. My outfit of choice for this bar included a pair of cowboy boots, button-fly Levi's, and a form-fitting tank top or T-shirt to show off my muscles. I never wore jewelry, though I will admit to wearing Jovan Musk Oil or Ralph Lauren's Polo on occasion. This was about 1982, so I even put a little pouf in my hair, and I made sure that the middle button on my Levi's was undone. At the edge of the dance floor, I stood with one cowboy boot carefully positioned in front of the other and my thumbs hanging inside my pockets.

The night we met, Alan was looking for a hot young man, and I was looking for business. Without saying a word, each of us knew where the other was coming from.

"Hi, how are you?" Alan said to me.

"Hello," I replied. Ever since high school, I could tell what a man's story was just by looking in his eyes. Alan's eyes appeared to be sincere.

"You sure are hot!" he said. "Would you like to dance?" I said sure, and we danced to a few songs.

Alan then asked, "How would you like to get together?"

"It starts at two hundred dollars," I told him. Confidence, kid, confidence. Next thing you know, Alan said, "It's a deal." He grabbed my hand, and off we went to dance some more.

Back then I didn't limit an encounter to just one hour. In fact, I would often let a client stay all night and sometimes let him buy me breakfast. Alan came over to my apartment, mostly because I did not care to go to a strange house. We got naked, had sex, and then fell asleep in each other's arms. In the morning, he got up, put on his urban cowboy clothes without taking a shower, paid me my money, and left.

Over the course of a year, Alan became my first regular client. He was fun to be with. He liked to dance to country-western music, and he really enjoyed lying in bed and talking. His money and his business were good, so I didn't mind having someone like him around.

I would learn over time that while it's good to have clients see you as a friend, you don't want to get too chummy with them because it will affect your judgment, and your business will suffer as a result. I learned to draw a distinct line between business and pleasure, as I did with Art, but in my early years I had no idea how to do that, and I sometimes wound up making friends instead of income.

After awhile, I started to see Alan in a nonsexual way. I stopped charging him and he stopped trying to get into my pants, and that was the start of a beautiful friendship. We would spend a lot of time together talking or watching movies. I was happy that things with him turned out the way they did. But once I started mixing business and friendship, as I did with Alan, my feelings about getting paid for getting laid got even more confused than they already were.

When you're young and horny all you want to do is have sex, so the fact that men seemed willing to line up to get naked with me was great. I can't think of a young man out there who wouldn't have liked that. But at the same time, I couldn't decide whether what I was doing was right or wrong—or even exactly what it was that I was doing. Was I going out looking for sex, or was I going out trying to make money? I was doing both, but I was confused about it. About the only thing I could be sure about was that the money I was making turning tricks was much better and easier than working as a busboy or an apprentice somewhere.

Another one of my first clients also wound up becoming a friend. Father Thomas was a Roman Catholic priest and still is to this day. Of course, I'm not using his real name. The archdiocese would fire him in a heartbeat—and then hit him up for my phone number.

I was working as a bartender at a 3.2 club, a nightclub for

the eighteen to twenty-one crowd who could only drink beer that had 3.2 percent alcohol. This good-looking man came in and sat down right in front of me, drinking a beer while staring intently at my crotch, my ass, my biceps, and my face.

He was infatuated from the start, but it was all based on my looks. When he asked me out, I told him I didn't do it for free. He said, "Fine, what's your price?" I told him, "It starts at two hundred dollars." Before long we had an appointment for Friday night.

He came back that Friday and waited patiently for me until I was done closing the bar. We went to my place and got frisky, and then, in the afterglow, he decided to tell me that he was a Roman Catholic priest.

I didn't grow up Catholic, but coming from a civic-minded family, I learned to have a lot of respect for men of the cloth. He told me to relax and treat him like I would any other man, but throughout our friendship, I found that hard to do. Here was a religious man, a man who was supposed to know more than most and be a role model, and we just got done doing the big nasty in my water bed. I admit I enjoyed the seediness of it all, but I wondered if this was the sin that would send me straight to hell.

He came to see me several more times. Back then, I wasn't charging by the hour, so he'd stay in my bed all night. I soon learned that he lived in a house with seven other priests, and he was the one in charge. By staying with me, he could have sex and get away from the parish for a while. He fell asleep so quickly after sex, it was probably also the only decent sleep he could get.

"You know, Jones, you're a great kid," he always told me. He was older and worldly, and I've always been attracted to that in men. I was young and, I guess, naïve, and for a caregiver like him, I was the perfect companion.

Sometimes we'd go to the rectory and be intimate right there in his bedroom, as Jesus on the cross watched over us. I wasn't tripped out about that as much as I was concerned that one of the other priests would say something. They all apparently knew we were having sex and that I was staying the night.

One time, while we walked, I figured I'd ask him a question that had been on my mind for some time: "Why is it that when good things happen, people thank God, but when bad things happen, they never blame him?" I told Thomas that my parents weren't religious, but that I had always heard many people praise Jesus for their good fortune. Yet when someone died or was the victim of crime, I never once heard God being cursed.

Thomas smiled at me, stopping momentarily. "I don't have an answer for you," he said softly. "I could make up an answer, but your question is valid, and I don't want to blow it off by dreaming up something to say."

One year, he asked if he could spend Christmas with me. I told him I was going to my grandmother's house, but I'd ask her if I could bring a friend. Always the hostess, she said of course. When I mentioned that my friend was a Catholic priest, I almost immediately regretted telling her what Thomas did for a living.

Come Christmas dinner, my grandmother was very nervous. She was trying so hard to get the place to look perfect, you'd think the pope was visiting. To her surprise, Thomas showed up wearing jeans and a polo shirt—not a priest's collar. Once she saw him, my grandmother became more relaxed. We had a great time.

After about six months, we stopped having sex but still enjoyed sharing afternoons or evenings. Our friendship came with some very nice perks. One time, he flew me to New Orleans for Mardi Gras, and we had a great time. Then there was the time I went to Rome, and he arranged for me to take a private tour of the Vatican. I soon learned that his name was almost as good as the pope's for unlocking doors.

Yet as time went on, it became apparent how much of an alcohol problem he had. He could put away vast quantities of beer and anything else that was around. I figured he drank a lot because he was lonely and kept such a busy schedule. I could only imagine what the demands on his time were: meetings with the bishop, masses every morning, visiting the sick, lecturing the novices, and then back home to read the Holy Book. Or maybe he was dealing with the fact that, according to the Vatican, he was considered "objectively disordered." If I had to deal with all that, I'd need a release, too.

I kept seeing Father Thomas until he was transferred out of the Denver area. We still talk by phone at least once every few months, two of those dates being my birthday and Christmas.

By the time I turned twenty-one and became a legal adult, I'd begun to piece together a better understanding of what I was doing. Altogether, the pieces amounted to nothing short of a revelation as far as I was concerned: in just three years, I'd been paid more than a hundred times to get naked with another man. Almost all of my clients had a need to be with someone like me, to make a connection that they'd always wanted but for some reason couldn't find. True to the American spirit, these men decided that the best way to get what they desired was to buy it. When they did, they felt better. If they felt better, that usually meant life was better. It was all pretty simple, really. I provided a much-needed service, and I was paid fair market value.

Yet something in the back of my mind told me to be careful. What I was doing wasn't wrong, but maybe it wasn't exactly right either. I couldn't explain what the gray area was, but it was there, and I thought about it constantly. At the same time, I tried not to let it interfere with my business. I remember thinking, *this can't last forever, because who will want to pay me for sex when I'm forty?*

Even as a legal adult, I had no idea how far to go with escorting. I saw myself looking more like a man and less like a young man, and I was certain that this would affect my ability to attract clients. In fact, it did affect things: it made me even more popular. I told everyone who asked, "It starts at two hundred dollars." I started putting ads in the yellow section, which was the adult section, of the local gay paper, advertising for "companionship." A few years later, I started taking out ads in gay papers in a variety of cities. "If you are looking to be pleasured, I know how to pleasure a man," one of my ads read.

I was still trying to go to college and figure out what I wanted to do with my life. I studied accounting at a community college in downtown Denver, but I found it increasingly difficult and stopped after awhile. When I was kid, a metal door fell on me, knocking me out cold. A few years after that, I was a batboy for a Little League team that my father was coaching. I wasn't paying attention, and I walked into the batter's box, only to have a kid warming up crack me right in the head with two baseball bats. It was an accident, but it, too, knocked me out cold. Ever since then, I have suffered from incredible migraines. Studying something such as accounting proved next to impossible for me.

I also had a variety of jobs that were nothing more than jobs. One I truly enjoyed was with the Rocky Mountain Adoption Exchange. Bringing adoptive parents and children together made me feel that I was doing something important, even if I was just handling the paperwork. By the time I turned forty, I had owned a bar and a greeting card shop. All of it was interesting and sometimes fun, but I still found myself escorting.

"Escorting," not "prostituting myself," pretty well sums up what I did, because while it involved my getting naked and sensual with someone, it wasn't at all what you might think. Sometimes I would just shampoo and bathe a client. Others wanted me to smoke a cigar while we got down and dirty. One guy, a pilot, wanted intimacy right there in his two-seater. Many people have the mistaken notion that when two guys get together for sex, it is raw, hard-core, butt-fucking activity. In reality, what stands out about the sex act is often anything but sex.

One time when I was new and on an outcall, I met a guy at his motel, the kind where the rooms are accessible from the parking lot. He was in his midforties, a truck driver, I believe, who was a bit heavyset. He greeted me at the door wearing just an open shirt and his underwear. I came into the room, and he offered me something from the many bottles of booze he had on display on the dresser. I asked for a bourbon and water. He prepared it in one of those small plastic motel cups that is individually shrink-wrapped. Fortunately, I was still fully clothed when my head started to buzz wildly. He had slipped me a Mickey, possibly GHB, a date-rape drug. I felt like I was going to collapse, but I was able to get up and leave, making my way safely to my car. I don't remember getting home and he certainly didn't pay me, but he didn't chase me and I got out of there unharmed, so I felt fortunate. I knew, though, that I was lucky; his buddies could have been waiting for me right outside his door.

I told Art about one client named Corky, who had to have been in his nineties.

"You've had sex with a ninety-year-old guy?" Art asked.

"It wasn't really sex," I replied. "He just wanted to be touched. He wore Coke-bottle glasses and was just a frail little thing."

Art twisted the cap on his bottle of water. "Could he . . . You know?"

"You mean, could he get it up?" Art nodded. "No, but that didn't matter. He came for the touch."

". . . Of another man?" Art asked.

"A lot of men need that," I replied. "Then there was this blind guy . . ."

Art smiled and leaned forward to listen more intently.

I told him how this blind man showed up for his appointment with his guide dog, which stayed with us in the massage room during the session. "You could tell this guy was really into touch. When he touched me it was like he was reading a book.

"I was amazed at how clearly he saw me through his fingertips and how well he got to know my personality by talking to me."

Art was entranced by my stories. "So it's not all sex," he stated.

"I recently had a client with lots of problems from diabetes," I said. I told him how over the course of our visits, he lost one leg and then the other. Art seemed amazed that I would see clients like that.

"I wasn't able to massage the stumps of his legs, though,"

I admitted. "So you see, I'm not Mother Teresa." We both laughed. At that moment Art and I were just like friends in an intimate coffee klatch.

"Have you ever had any weirdo clients?"

One time in 1995, I had a very good-looking client come see me. During our session, all he wanted to do was talk. "This guy talked nonstop, and it was getting annoying," I said in a storytelling voice.

He asked me if escorting was the only kind of work I did. Foolishly, I told him not only that I had another job, but also the name of the company where I worked. He kept asking personal questions, and I tried my best to blow them off. He then seemed to calm down and didn't pursue anything further. When the session ended, he paid me and was on his way.

The next day, I arrived at my job at eight o'clock as usual. I entered through the building's back door, which was the entrance employees used, and went to my desk. Within moments, I received a call from the receptionist, who told me that there was someone up front to see me. I asked who it was, and she said he would not give his name.

I told her I would come up front in a few minutes. Given that the company I worked for serviced loans, it could have been anyone. Still, I was not expecting anyone that day, so I went to a door near the waiting area and peeked out.

I could not believe it. It was the client from the night before. I was stunned. I went back to my desk, called the receptionist, and told her to tell the visitor that I had to go to a meeting and would be tied up for hours.

What did this guy want? Why would he come to where I worked? My mind raced. As luck would have it, this guy wound up waiting for me in the lobby the entire day. As employees wearing badges passed him, he told them that he was not going to leave until he could give me an envelope.

I was really nervous. Should I call the police? He was dressed in a three-piece suit, so everyone probably thought he was there to serve me papers. Fortunately, my boss never asked me anything about it.

Come five o'clock, the building was closing, and I decided to walk out with the flow of employees, hoping to mingle in. But as I tried to escape, he saw me, handed me an envelope, and left the building.

I was shaken. I went home and read the contents of the envelope. It was a torrid three-page letter about how much he loved me and wanted to be with me for the rest of his life. He added that he would do anything for me.

"I threw the letter away," I told Art. "For the next several weeks, I lived in fear that he would show up at work to bother me again."

"That's creepy!" Art replied. "Have you had any clients who died of AIDS?"

"One of my very first clients died recently. I'm not sure what the cause of death was. It might have been suicide, I don't know." My eyes began to water.

Art put his hand on mine. "What was his name?"

It was Alan, the professor I met at the country-western bar. I told Art how he couldn't seem to find happiness once he turned sixty-five, how he had given up on the gay community and seemed to have given up on life itself. I told Art how, one night, Alan and I were drinking wine and listening to classical music when Alan suddenly started talking about killing himself.

"I talked him out of it and encouraged him to get some help," I told Art. "Things got better for awhile. But a few months later, I learned from a mutual friend that Alan had been diagnosed with throat cancer. I tried to see him, but he kept me away. Then I heard he had died. I want to believe that the cause was cancer, but I have my doubts." I didn't know what to say next, so I just said, "I meet a lot of very wonderful people doing what I do."

"I hope to be one of your memorable clients," Art replied. With that, he stood up, gave me a hug, and headed out the door.

It was rare for me to take that much time to talk to a client. He had wanted to talk, and I had wanted to talk. The subject matter was life, and for two men who barely knew each other, it was pretty deep.

I looked at the clock and noticed that even with our conversation, Art had been in my place for only a little more than an hour. That's my kind of client!

CHAPTER 3

MY SECOND YEAR WITH ART

□

"Hey, Mike, I'm running late, but I should be there in fifteen minutes or so. Okay? Bye." I erased the voice-mail message and went to the kitchen to tidy up. There were only a few glasses in the sink so it didn't take long.

I had recently moved from the condo on Sherman Street to an apartment on Downing Street and had also given up the studio next door to the condo. Since then, I had been entertaining clients in my new place. It was important to me that the apartment look neat—although I'm not sure that anyone who ever came to my place cared about how the kitchen looked.

My next stop was the bathroom. I usually took a minute to wipe down the toilet rim, sink, and counters. Again, I don't ever recall anyone commenting on how clean my bathroom was, but I knew that if it looked like a guy's bathroom, stench and all, someone would have said something. On the counter, I made sure I had plenty of mouthwash, paper cups, fresh combs, toothpaste, shaving cream, and a roll of paper towels. I've found that men do better with paper towels than with a nice set of hand towels. It works for me, too, since it means less laundry to do.

I then went to the bedroom to straighten up, but that was just for my own satisfaction. I very rarely brought anyone into the bedroom. For starters, that was my space, and it was important to keep at least one room in the apartment as mine. More importantly, however, a bed just presented too many issues. Once my career really got going, I let almost no one stay more than one hour and often had to say no to clients who wanted to stay the night, even if they were ready to pay me for eight hours.

"Mike, I'm here," Art said. I buzzed him in and told him to come to the eighth floor. He hadn't been to my new place yet. It was in a tall apartment building right in the heart of Capitol Hill in central Denver, a neighborhood where a lot of gay men and other creative types live.

Two minutes later, with a quick, almost gentle knock on the front door, Art was ready for action.

"Hi, Mike," he said with a wide grin. "God, I've missed you."

He stood at the door until I gestured for him to come in. "Hello, Art," I said. He was now trying to kiss me on the lips whenever he could, but I always turned my cheek toward him. Art rubbed my shoulders and my chest.

"Why the new place?" he asked.

"I got tired of the home owner's association." That was true, really.

Before going into the massage room to undress, I gave Art a glass of water. Everything was quiet, just the way he liked it, though there was a bit more noise coming from the street.

Art loved rubbing my chest, moving his hands up and down firmly. After his fingers did the walking on my clean-shaven chest, he put his hand on the small of my back and pulled me in toward him. You could almost feel the passion in his face as he closed his eyes, clenched his teeth ever so slightly, and then held on to me for dear life.

He clenched my hand again, gave me a squeeze, and then let go. He went into the massage room to get undressed.

After a few minutes, I walked in and took off my gym shorts. Rather than wait for me on his stomach, Art was standing with a full erection. When I approached, he kissed my neck, cheeks, and forehead, all the while rubbing my chest, biceps, and abdomen. His hands worked their way down my body until he got to my pubic area. His touch suggested both delight and trepidation.

In one smooth gliding motion, his hands cupped my groin, and he effortlessly dropped to his knees in front of me, lightly breathing on me all the while. Sometimes we'd do it standing, and sometimes he'd place me in a chair and let me sit back and relax while he did all the work. His joy at doing this was obvious.

"Let me massage you," I told him softly. I then guided him onto the table and began our usual routine. Once again, he tried to perform oral sex but couldn't quite do it. No matter. I rubbed him down, flipped him over, and helped him ejaculate. That remained a regular part of our routine.

"Man, I like your chest," he commented as he lay on his back, rubbing my pectoral muscles. "How did you get it so big and hard?"

I smiled and rubbed his thigh. "Do you want all the details?"

Art smiled and didn't say anything more. He didn't really want the details. Like someone on the first day at school or work, he was just making conversation. Even after a year of monthly visits he was still hesitant. He wanted to do more than touch me, to be sure. He wanted to make a connection. But he still wasn't sure how.

As usual, once he had his release, it took less than five minutes for him to get up, get changed, and be on his way. "I feel like I can trust you," he told me that day as he handed me the money. I didn't think much of his comment until the next time he came to visit.

Art's eyes were piercing, so much so that they sometimes felt like a needle sticking in me. His eyebrows told both of his pleasure and of his anticipation of where our adventures would take him. Sometimes his face signaled a heightened sense of pleasure. Sometimes his face showed fear, as though he were in need of being rescued.

"Are there still massage parlors?" Art asked as we played.

"Are you thinking of visiting one?" I asked. I wasn't trying to be mean, I just didn't know how to respond to what seemed like an odd question.

"Are there any swingers' hotels around here?"

Since he was seemingly in the mood to talk, I obliged him. "There's an interesting one farther down on East Colfax."

Two Roman Catholic priests had hired me once for an afternoon of play at this gated establishment, where you were charged by the hour with no questions asked. I met these two men, both in their forties, inside the room, which was adorned in jungle red. There were mirrored ceilings, oversized beds, jungle gyms, harnesses, slings—and all kinds of toiletries in the bathroom to use before going to your next appointment. The two priests and I did little more than get naked and touch each other for mild stimulation. An hour later, it was over. I got paid, and I never saw either of them again.

"I think you'd enjoy it," I offered. "Anything else you want to know, big boy?"

Art had a quizzical look on his face. *Oh dear*, I thought. *Was I about to become his sex therapist?*

Before he could speak, I reached down and felt his erection. "Let's flip you over," I said, hoping to steer him away from whatever train of thought he was riding. I jacked him off, gave him a towel, and left him in the massage room by himself. He took a little longer than usual to get to the bathroom to change. Maybe he was thinking of trying other venues besides me.

Another time, Art sat on the couch after he arrived, watching my every movement.

"Wow!" he sighed, admiring my physique.

Wearing not a stitch of clothing, I stood in front of him and flexed every muscle. I did the classic bicep flex pose. I also did the "which way to the beach" pose. I clasped my hands together and pumped my arms for him.

"You look just like Arnold Schwarzenegger!" he said.

"How 'bout Charles Atlas?" I asked. I never thought Arnold was all that attractive.

I moved toward him and put my muscles—every muscle— right in his face. As usual, he didn't remove his clothes or touch himself while we were out in the living room. The most he would do was rub the crotch of his jeans.

"You like my big muscles, big boy?"

He smiled and replied, "I think I'm ready." He got up and went to the massage room to get undressed. While I waited, I took a sip of water. Posing is hard work. Laying him on his back and jacking him off was much easier.

Waiting on the massage table, Art was chatty again.

"Have you ever had any strange requests?"

As I rubbed lotion on his back, I told him about this one guy who had a shoe fetish. "He said he was from Minnesota, and right in the middle of being naked, he said, 'Hey, can I ask you something?' I said sure, so he asked me if I had a pair of cowboy boots and would I mind wearing them while I massaged him?

"Turns out, I did have a pair of black cowboy boots, so I put on a pair of socks and the boots, and there I was, buck naked, wearing just the boots and a smile."

Art wasn't paying attention so I cut the story short.

"I get a lot of interesting requests," I said. "If I can fulfill them, I do. If I can't, I say so."

Art sighed as I rubbed his butt. "That's good to know," he replied. Really, what could he possibly ask me that I hadn't already heard?

"Thank you, Mike," Art said at the end of a different visit, just having finished doing what he came to do. Lying on his back, he very calmly looked up to the ceiling and said, "Hey, Mike, can I ask you something?"

I figured he wanted to try something a little kinkier, or maybe he had questions about HIV and STDs. If so, I was ready to refer him to some medical people I knew.

Imagine my surprise when Art asked calmly, "What do you know about meth?"

I wasn't prepared for that one. In all my years being an escort, I had never had anyone ask me about drugs. Sure, many men showed up obviously high, drunk, or tweaking. I suppose I shouldn't have been caught off guard, but Art seemed like such a clean-cut guy.

"It's not really my thing," I replied, as calmly as I could, touching his arm.

"Really?" Art replied.

"I don't care for it personally, but I have friends that do it." Oh boy, what have I gotten myself into?

"So you've done it?" he asked, with deep anticipation of my answer in his voice.

"Yes," I replied, "a few times." By this point, I'd known

Art for over a year, so I had no reason to think this was a setup, but that thought still goes through your mind when you're in the business. "Like I said, I didn't care for it." I really wanted to emphasize that point to make sure he got it.

"Your friends, why do they like it?"

Is this guy really that naïve or is he fishing for something? "They say it enhances their sexual pleasure. I guess it just makes you less inhibited, especially if you are doing something you feel you shouldn't be doing." Ouch, did I really say that to Art?

"Do you know where I can get some?" he asked.

I paused and thought a moment, nervously. "I don't deal, if that's what you're asking." I had to get that in there, figuring that if there was a bug somewhere, that had better be part of the tape.

"I'd just like to try some." I wondered where he got the idea that crystal meth would be worth trying. "Can you hook me up?"

Picture the best day of your life when everything is going right. You just hit the lottery, you just had a brand new beautiful baby, and nothing could seem better than that moment in life. That's what it can feel like the first time you use meth. It's a sex drug. It can make you feel euphoric or paranoid, energetic or sleep deprived, but its effect can go in either direction.

Methamphetamine doesn't occur naturally, like cocaine or marijuana. It's a synthetic nervous-system stimulant. For the casual user, it can enhance sexual pleasure, but for the addict, it can control and ruin lives.

I still had no reason to think this was a setup, but my instincts for self-preservation were kicking in hard. "I'll ask around," I replied. "I'll see what I can do." I had little interest in pursuing his request. We were done for the day, so, as usual, he became silent, scurried to the bathroom with his clothes in hand, came out a few minutes later, paid me, kissed me on the cheek, and left.

It was true that I had tried meth and equally true that I didn't care for it. I was at a friend's house a few years back, and there were four of us who got naked and had fun. They had some meth and told me how it heightens the sexual experience, so I figured I'd try some. I enjoyed it for the first few hours. I experienced a type of euphoria that made me forget my problems and hang-ups.

It was great until I tried to go to sleep later that night and couldn't. In fact, because of the meth, I was awake for three days straight, no matter how hard I tried to collapse. You can imagine what a wreck I was when I finally did collapse. After that, I decided the temporary euphoria I got from meth wasn't worth the problems I would have days later.

I thought about telling Art this, but as with all my clients, I really felt it was not my concern, nor did I want to make it my concern.

Later that month, another client I had seen before called to book an appointment. I remembered from a previous conversation that he enjoyed meth. I had no reason to think he knew anything more about meth than using it occasionally, but I figured I'd ask. Perhaps I should have told Art no. Not that I would impose on anyone any of my own opinions of meth, but, God, what a hassle. Talk about going the extra mile for your clients!

So when my other client, let's call him Todd, arrived for his appointment, I waited until the end of the session to tell him about Art and his request. "If you don't mind, can I have him call you?"

"How long have you known this guy?" Todd asked pointedly.

"About a year. I believe he is trustworthy," I assured Todd.

"Okay, then why don't you have Art call me, and I'll talk to him and see what we can do." Todd added, "Tell him to make sure he mentions your name so I'll know who he is."

I thanked Todd and he left.

The next time I saw Art, he barely got in the door and kissed me before asking, "Did you get any meth?" His eyes were wide, his brows were wider, and all his pearly whites and molars were on display. I couldn't believe how excited he was about getting started on this new adventure.

"Let me give you a phone number," I said as I wrote Todd's number down on a sticky note and handed it to him.

Art's face suddenly went sour. "I thought you were going to have some here . . . today." He wasn't mean about it, but he was starting to act like a disappointed child on Christmas.

"Art," I said calmly, "I told you I don't deal in any kind of drugs." Thinking in my usual cautious way, I added, "I don't have any drugs on me, and I don't keep any here at the house." Sure, I was being overly cautious. But why take any chances?

Seeing the huge disappointment in his eyes, I felt I needed to turn his mood around—and quickly. "Let's watch some porn," I said. Then I rubbed his hair playfully, just like a father would rub his son's head. "Now give Todd a call and see . . . see if he can help you, okay?"

The smile returned to Art's face as I guided him to the couch. I popped a DVD in the player, and we both sat down to watch *Bare Muscle: Thick and Raw.*

If you are into real men having heart-stopping, hard-pounding man-sex with no-holds-barred, then BARE

MUSCLE is going to be the next video to add to your collection . . .

Art was beginning to take a shine to porn. He and I rubbed each other as we sat on the couch. He was still fully clothed, and I wore nothing but my gym shorts. As the action on-screen heated up, I could tell that Art was starting to loosen up, though he did say, "I sure would like to have some meth right now." His obsession seemed odd because I was under the impression that he'd never tried it before, but maybe he had gotten a hold of some since then.

As soon as he was aroused, Art went to the massage room to get ready. I waited a few minutes, then took off my shorts and went in. I rubbed him all over, as usual.

The visit, however, was notable because he had difficulty reaching climax. I could tell he was trying, but no matter what he did, nothing seemed to be working. At one point, I could tell he had simply given up. His body dropped back into the massage table in frustration.

"It's okay, handsome," I assured him.

He lay there in silence, angry at himself, but for what, I wasn't sure.

"Hey, Art, it's okay!"

Visibly rattled, Art hopped off the massage table without wiping himself off. As usual, he grabbed his clothes and ran to the bathroom. Before I could think of anything to say, he was out the door, with barely a good-bye or a thank you on the way out.

His next visit proved to be more challenging.

"Look what I have," he said smiling, ecstatic beyond belief.

I couldn't believe it, really. There he was, barely inside my door, waving a small packet of what I assumed was meth.

"I can't wait to try this," he said immediately, going for one of the two chairs at my dining-room table. "How do you do this?"

You have got to be kidding, I thought. I was truly starting to consider the possibility that I was being set up, but in this business your best gauge is your gut, and my gut was telling me that Art was still a harmless guy who knew so little about the world that he couldn't even figure out how to get high. I cleared my throat and took a seat across from him at my table.

"What do you mean, 'how do you do this'?" I asked, carefully.

"How do you use this?" he asked again, opening the packet.

I was starting to get nervous. I never had any client use drugs in my presence, and I was getting very nervous about such an obvious display of meth, or whatever it was, right in my apartment. I still felt Art was harmless, but he was becoming more like one of those naïve and clumsy clients that can easily get you and everyone else into trouble.

I rubbed my face feverishly. "Do you have a dollar bill?" Art looked at me curiously.

"It's not for my tip, it's for the meth," I assured him. He smiled and pulled out a crisp, stiff dollar bill. I took it from him, and with the cap from a ball-point pen, I scooped out a very small amount of the white crystals. I also asked him for a credit card so I could crush the crystals, which can be chunky and hard. I told him to form it into a line, no more than one inch in length. "You really have to be careful with this stuff! You can't play around with it!" I almost yelled, only to turn around and say, "I'm sorry."

Art reached over for my arm. "Does this upset you?" he asked in a very sincere tone.

Quickly regaining my composure, I finished smoothing out the line of meth and then rolled the dollar bill carefully so it could work as a straw. "You simply put one end of the dollar bill to the meth and the other end inside your nose and inhale." I simulated how to do it without putting the bill into the meth or putting it inside my nostril. "Be sure to do it slowly. If you have any difficulty, just stop," I instructed.

Art's glow was starting to fade a bit. Perhaps he was starting to see that this was not as glamorous as he had envisioned. He carefully took the tightly rolled bill from my hands and put it inside his nostril as far as it could go. He then leaned over the table and placed the other end of the bill right into the meth. But instead of inhaling, he exhaled, causing the line to move a bit. "Sorry," he said.

He pulled back from the meth, exhaled slightly, and then bent down over the line of meth again. Carefully, he inhaled, taking small amounts of meth into the dollar bill.

"That's enough!" I shouted suddenly. Maybe I shouldn't have done that, but I wanted him to go slow and not try to do it all in one snort. "I'm sorry," I said. "I just want you to take your time."

"It's all right, Mike." He took another small snort through the dollar bill to finish the line, paused, and then sat up. He didn't have much of reaction, really, other than saying, "It burns." No shit, but I told him the burn should go away in a few seconds. He sat there, somewhat dazed, or maybe he was just waiting for something to happen.

"What do you think?" I asked.

Art shrugged a bit. "Not bad," he said. "Maybe a little more?"

"I would not do more," I warned. "Give it a few minutes."

I thought about a client who started having serious chest

pains right in the middle of our session. He was much older than Art. The guy finally said, "I think you better call an ambulance," so I did. Before medical help arrived, I had gotten him dressed so there would be few questions about what led up to the chest pains. Once in my apartment, the EMS crew asked me questions that I couldn't answer. I told them that I had just met this gentleman and I knew nothing about him. One of them then started looking around my apartment and came across a bottle of pills. "What's this?" he asked. I told him it was Cialis, a brand-new drug at the time, and that you take it to get hard. He put down the bottle and asked me no further questions, following the rest of the paramedics out the door with my client on a stretcher. No illegal drugs were involved, to my knowledge.

As the meth kicked in, Art's expression went all over the place, but overall, he looked happy, at times even euphoric.

"How are you doing?" I asked.

"Fine, thank you," he replied, somewhat glassy eyed. "Just fine."

Nervous about him overdoing it, I offered to take him directly to the massage room.

"That would be nice," he said, still seeming somewhat disconnected. I grabbed his hand from across the table and helped him stand up.

As I pulled him away from the table, however, he pulled on my shoulders and wanted to French-kiss me. I was not turned on by this, and was even more turned off by the trace of meth that was underneath his right nostril.

"Let's get naked!" I told him quickly. I already had the massage room ready to go with just one candle. I got him in the room, shut the door, and to my surprise, he took off his clothes with me standing right there. That was the first time he ever undressed in front of me. With a noticeable increase in aggression, he tried to kiss me again and then put his hands down my shorts.

"Art!" I exclaimed as he squeezed me hard. He wasn't acting high or weird, just more intense. He was hugging me so tight, it was almost as if he wanted to crawl inside me or get inside me somehow. I guided him to the massage table and told him to lie down. That worked for a few minutes, but Art was clearly too wound up. I helped him up and moved him to one of the chairs nearby. He sat in it for a few minutes while I played with him, but then he got up and sat me in the chair so he could kneel in front of me.

There was a big difference in Art after he took the meth. It was as if suddenly all his inhibitions were gone and he was ready to do everything he'd ever fantasized about. His motions, his breathing—everything was more intense. Yes, it concerned me, but I'd seen it before in clients, and I knew that I had nothing to fear. Art was complex, but a tendency towards violence was never one of his character traits.

When I looked at Art, I saw a lot more than just the color of his eyes. It was as if Art were a puzzle with several hundred pieces. Just by looking at the pieces, no obvious pattern emerged. You could put the border of the puzzle together, but you could not be sure that every piece would fit.

He was quiet, to be sure, and when he spoke, he said little. He was never boastful, and there was always a sense of shame, guilt, or something that was not right with him. He wasn't looking just to get his rocks off. He wanted more. He needed more. I just couldn't tell what it was.

As we stood crotch-to-crotch, I was able to get him off. His body became the most intense I had ever seen it, but after the moment was over, he almost collapsed in my arms. Carefully, I guided him down to a chair so he could cool off.

"Thank you, Mike," he panted. "I've never done anything like that before."

No shit. I watched him carefully until his breathing came back to normal. I put a towel on his groin and held it there. He was still excited, but I tried not to think if that was natural or chemical.

A few minutes later, he grabbed his clothes and went to the bathroom. I was thoroughly exhausted from our session. I started to strip the massage table and prepare the room for the next client.

Standing in the living room, I watched Art come out of the bathroom with wet hair and wearing a slightly wrinkled shirt. Suddenly, the joy and intensity were gone. He looked like he was going to cry.

I gave him a bear hug. "Thanks for coming, Art."

He hugged me back hard, as though he were holding on for dear life. "Thank you, Mike. I really enjoyed it." He handed me two hundred-dollar bills and a little extra. I could tell he was sad.

I gave him another hug and watched him walk down the hall to the elevator. I then quickly cleaned any residue of meth off my table. I washed my hands very thoroughly, repeatedly. I wanted no trace of meth anywhere in the house.

Every time he came over after that, he did a little meth—I assume it was meth—before we got naked. One time he asked me if you could mix meth with a joint. I told him I didn't know, but I supposed you could. I suggested he look for someone who was more knowledgeable. He also asked me about ecstasy, and I told him I had had only one experience with it, but I felt it was overrated and usually taken by people who want to dance all night.

When he came over, Art would sit at my dining room table

to prepare his meth and take it there. One time, as he got his meth ready, he was particularly chatty.

"You know what?" he said. "I love doing this stuff before I have sex with my wife."

If I was supposed to be shocked, I wasn't. I didn't say anything and just acted like I didn't hear him.

Art gave himself a minute for everything to kick in, and then he met me inside the massage room. For Art, it was naked fun and games from there.

I had a chest full of sex toys that I kept for my clients to use and enjoy. There were sessions now when Art played with one toy after another. Sometime he knew what they were and how they were used, and sometimes he didn't. He asked a lot of questions, and I saw that as a good sign. It's easy to injure yourself with a pair of tit clamps if you are not careful.

Shortly after meth became part of his routine, Art started carrying a small canvas bag with a variety of his own adult toys and accessories. In a short period of time, he had accumulated a lot of them: cock rings made of leather, rubber, or metal; jockstraps; tit clamps; and porn that he wanted to watch.

"Look at what I bought!" he'd say as he showed me the latest addition to his collection.

"Hey, Mike, can I ask you something?"

I nodded.

"Do you know any young college guys?"

I said, "I know some. Why?"

"I think it would be hot to have sex with a bunch of athletic young studs."

I scratched my head, mostly because I was really hoping he wouldn't pursue it any further.

"Do you think you could arrange something like that?"

"Let me look into it," I said. I gave him a quick hug and took him into the massage room. We had a typical session that time. On his way out the door, Art reminded me that he'd really like to meet some young college guys.

I made a few phone calls, but it wasn't looking good. The next time he called, the first thing he asked was how the orgy was coming along. I told him I was still working on it. But a few days later, when Art called again, I told him that the orgy was not going to happen because I couldn't get enough guys together.

"Oh, shoot. Well, thanks for trying," Art said, disappointed.

"Maybe we can try again later," I offered.

When Art arrived for his next appointment, he did his usual hit of meth. "Tell me about these guys that were going to come over," Art asked eagerly as he got on the massage table.

"Oh, the ones I know are quite handsome," I told him. "Hot, young, hung, horny. You would have liked them." As we played with each other, I told Art about five young studs, around twenty-two years of age, three with blonde hair and blue eyes, the other two with brown hair and brown eyes.

"Mike, do you know what would really turn me on? I would love to watch you and another hot bodybuilder get it on."

I kept the passion going, trying not to think too much about what he was saying.

"I don't want to participate, but I would love to watch. Could you arrange that?"

I told him it would be double because I'd have to pay my "buddy." Art said okay, and we continued with our passion.

I called a friend named Matt and asked if he would like to make an easy hundred dollars. "It will probably take less than half an hour," I assured him. Matt said no problem.

"Art, I'd like you to meet Matt."

Art extended his right hand to shake Matt's, moving his eyes up and down Matt's physique. "Very nice to meet you," he said in an anxious tone.

Matt was a handsome, sturdy young man with a body-builder's physique. Wearing just a jockstrap and a little body lotion, his stance was statuesque and his looks solidly masculine.

"Are you ready to see us get it on?" I asked Art in a rough, sexy voice.

Art nodded his head and took a seat on a chair. This all happened by the light of just one tea candle. I waited a few moments while Art got situated. I didn't know if he was undressing or unzipping or what he was doing. While we waited, I started playing with Matt, snapping his jockstraps in a combination of foreplay and horseplay. That session may have been the first time Art had ever been with two other men.

"I'm ready," Art whispered. "Show me some hot sex."

Okay, show time. "You want my big fucking dick?" I said to Matt in a dominating tone. It was all role-playing for us, because Matt and I had been friends for years, and we had never talked to each other like that.

"Sir, can I have it?" Matt begged.

Art seemed to be enjoying it, though it was hard to tell. In reality, I just wanted to get the show over with.

Matt and I kept up the nasty talk because Art seemed to really respond to it. Sensing that perhaps he wanted to see a little bit of tenderness, Matt and I slowed it down and rubbed each other sensually.

"Oh, yeah!" Art whispered.

From that point on, the show was a combination of hot man-on-man action and sensual lovemaking. We tried to do whatever Art seemed to respond to.

It may have seemed impromptu, but for Matt and me it was all choreographed. I've seen lots of gay porn movies, so I knew how things were supposed to end after two guys had hot and heavy sex with each other. That's what Art wanted, I knew.

"Yeah, Daddy, give it to me!" Matt moaned, his naked body silhouetted on the wall. We had discussed earlier how Art wanted to see Matt reach his peak, so I told Matt not to prolong it, to do it as soon as he was ready so we could all get out of there quicker. Within moments, all the action came to a climax, and then, with little more then a slap on the thigh, it ended. I said thank you and Matt said thank you, and then we both stood up as though we were going to take a bow.

I could hear Art moving about, so I assumed he was done with whatever he was doing. I gave him a moment to walk to the bathroom. Once I heard the bathroom door close, I blew out the tea candle, turned on the lights, and Matt and I got cleaned up. I gave Matt one hundred dollars and sent him on his way.

Since Art was ready to leave, I put on some gym shorts, gave him a hug, and wished him well as he left. I tidied up the massage room, put on a shirt and shoes, and headed down the street for some coffee.

"One guy hired me to spank him while his girlfriend watched," I told Art. "Two friends of mine, a gay couple, hired me to pose while one did a sketch of me and the other one got off on it. And once, I was even asked by a group of professional gay men to be a naked centerpiece on a table of food."

Art laughed as he rubbed my chest. "You've had an exciting life!"

I smiled. "I'm sure you've had some excitement in your life, too."

He sighed and said, "I ride a motorcycle, and that's about all the excitement I have going on right now."

During the warmer months, Art sometimes showed up at my door carrying a motorcycle helmet. It was solid black and had the letters DOT on it. I had no idea what they stood for, but they were big and obvious. *Could DOT be his initials?* I wondered. I did not ask him any questions about the bike. I am not a big fan of motorcycles. I know nothing about them, and I've lost two good friends to bike accidents. Still, it was no big deal to me that he rode one. My only concern was that he would do meth in my apartment and then hop on his bike an hour later.

"Just be careful when you ride," I told him. "You're too beautiful a man to get hurt like that."

Art's face lit up. "You really mean that, don't you?" he said.

"Of course I mean it, Art. You are a wonderful man." I had the feeling it meant more to him to hear that from me than from anyone else in the world.

He said nothing more, then gave me a big squeeze and left.

I guess I was still trying to bring him out of his shell. Even though I knew that might never happen, I thought I could still make him feel like the sexiest man on earth.

I got a call from a young man who wanted to see me while he was on vacation in Colorado for six weeks. I said sure and scheduled an appointment. Right on time, he rang my buzzer and came upstairs to my apartment.

He was a good-looking man, probably in his mid to late twenties. He was about six feet tall, 220 pounds, fairly muscular, and had one of the best postures I'd ever seen. That, and his high-and-tight haircut, told me he was in the military. You can spot U.S. military guys a mile away. Great posture, sharp looks, and the most gentlemanly manners you'll find anywhere. When Lowry Air Force Base was open, guys who were staying there on temporary duty would come see me.

I showed Roger (not his real name, of course) into the massage room, where he proceeded to take off his clothes. I got the massage lotion, the candles, and the music ready. Before I could say at ease, he was facedown on the massage table, totally nude. I love giving massages to military men. Their bodies are so hard and tight that they are usually perfect specimens of what the human body can be. Okay, it turns me on, too.

He didn't say much while he was on his stomach, even as I was massaging his butt. Once I rolled him over, he got chatty, so we started having a pretty lively conversation. He told me was staying in Golden, Colorado, "with family." That usually meant a wife and child, but it could have also meant his parents. I didn't really want to know.

Sensing that he wanted to keep the conversation going, I jumped in with what I thought was an innocuous question. "Are you enjoying your vacation here in Colorado?" I asked.

A moment later, tears started trickling down his cheeks. He didn't move, even to wipe his eyes. He just lay there, struggling with an emotional pain that was ready to burst.

"I'm not here on vacation," he told me as he reached for my hand. I leaned toward him a bit, turning my ear toward his face to show that I was listening. "I'm here for a few more weeks . . . and then I have to go back to Iraq."

How I hated to hear that. I've learned over the years to keep a cool poker face, even when one is not required, but I could almost feel my cool coming apart. I kept holding his hand as he talked.

"I've already been over there once," he said. Maybe he thought I was going to ask him something specific, because he quickly followed up with, "You don't want to know what I've been through."

I tried my best to muster a smile. I wanted so badly to tell him everything would be okay, but how could I tell him that? All I could do was hold his hand and, I don't know, *comfort* him, whatever that means. I was taken aback by what he was saying. Here was this good-looking young man coming to see me for comfort and joy before being sent back to the battle-field, and once he got there he could face a court martial if anyone found out what he and I had done back home.

So I cracked a smile and wound up saying "it's okay" any-way, even though I didn't want to say that. I leaned down over him and gave him a big bear hug, a powerful one where our chests pressed firmly against each other.

He was still crying. I almost felt like crying, too. I finished his massage, and then he wanted me to jack him off, which I did. The intensity in his body as he was getting ready to shoot was extreme. I don't recall ever having any man who became that intense. Once he was finished, I could almost see his ten-sions—and all his demons—leave his body. He was clearly exhausted and wound up falling asleep.

I let him lay there, unconcerned with time. With all the

stress he must have about going back to Iraq, being on a short vacation, and having homosexual tendencies, no wonder he was ready to explode. I wondered if he had a wife and kids and if he was getting ready to leave them, too. I admit I had to force back some tears as I watched him sleep. Suddenly, he began to look like he was lying in a casket, so I quickly woke him up.

"You okay, handsome?" I asked briskly as I shook him back to life.

He wiped his eyes, yawned, and stretched his arms and legs. "I'm good . . ."

"It's okay," I said again.

After a short pause, he got up from the table and got dressed. "Thank you, Mike," he said as he gave me my money. His eyes still had tears in them as he left. As I watched him walk down the hall to the elevator, I couldn't help but wonder if I would ever see him again. As it turns out, I did not see him again, but I hope that's because he's moved on to bigger and better things, not because he was killed.

CHAPTER 4

MY MOTHER, SHIRLEY JONES

▣

My parents met at a roller rink in the early 1950s when they were both still in high school. My father recalls being attracted to my mother's pretty and sincere face. The night they met, he was hanging out with his buddies and she was hanging out with her girlfriends. My mother attended Edgewater High School and my father attended rival Mountair High School. The conversation that night blossomed into a lifelong marriage and friendship. It was very apparent to me growing up that my parents loved each other very much.

After graduation, my father joined the Air Force to avoid being drafted into the Army. My mother was still in high school. While my father was on leave a year later, they decided to get married at a small ceremony at my grandmother Kaylor's house. My mother traveled wherever duty took him, having her first child, Russ, in 1954. She was not even eighteen when she first gave birth. Once my father got out of the Air Force, the family of three came back to Denver, and my father took a job at a lumber company where his father worked. After he had saved enough money, they bought a house in Edgewater.

And that's where my story begins, in a small sleepy suburb called Edgewater, just west of Denver. It's a lot like Mayberry, or any other small town of the 1950s you can imagine. There were only six thousand residents, but we had our own city government, with police and fire departments, a city council, a mayor, and a court house. Everyone knew everyone else. My mother caught wind that the mayor was looking to hire an officer. She encouraged my father to apply and spoke highly of him to the Edgewater movers and shakers. Before long, Dad was hired as Edgewater's first paid police officer.

The steady income was good, but now that my parents had two mouths to feed—me and Russ—their finances became strained. I was still quite small, maybe not even two, when my mother was hired by the Colorado Health Department as a receptionist.

My older brother Russ was already in school, and my younger brother Terry had not yet been born. Having no choice, my mother left me in the care of my great-grandmother during the day. Before I could develop a meaningful bond with my mother, I developed a deep connection to my great-grandmother Grace. To this day, I am grateful I had that opportunity.

My great-grandmother, Grace Dougherty, was born in Central City in 1890. You could say she was a true pioneer woman, as she grew up right in the middle of one of the largest mining booms in the nation's history. Miners, prospectors, merchants, thieves, and gold diggers had all descended on Central City for more than fifty years. They were all in search of minerals or whatever else might make them rich quickly.

Grace Dougherty was a good-looking woman, a brunette with doe eyes and a very sweet disposition. She was tall and lanky and loved getting all dolled up. She could be dainty, but she was also as tough as nails. She had to be to deal with all the roughnecks that inhabited Colorado's mountain towns at the time.

Grace worked at one of the nicest hotels in Central City, one that also had a reputation for having ladies of the night available. And my great-grandmother's job there included being a madam for the other girls, as well as doing some entertaining herself. No one in my family ever tried to hide the fact that she used to entertain clients there. At the same time, no one, including her, ever went into detail about it. It was a secret we shared, something that was embarrassing, I guess. I never understood that until I got older and learned that keeping secrets could be a way of life.

"Remember, she was the bookkeeper!" My grandmother Allene would always say that about her mother. To my knowledge, my great-grandmother, who I used to call "Nanny," didn't know a thing about accounting. All I knew was that she loved me and took care of me. At age three, what more is there?

My grandmother Allene, however, was a real bookkeeper and used to make a decent living back in an era when women weren't suppose to work for wages and benefits. They were both very strong women, as was my mother.

After her husband died, my Nanny moved in with her daughter, my grandmother Allene, and my grandfather Vernon. They lived in a house in Edgewater that seemed huge to me, even though it had only two bedrooms.

My great-grandmother was almost seventy years old when we shared afternoons together. In the 1960s, that was considered very old, but age never meant a thing to me, and anyway, she was young in spirit. The only time she showed her age was through her wisdom. Knowing what I know about her now, no wonder she was wise.

Nanny kept dozens of white carnations all around the house. Because of her, I developed an eye for beauty. That wasn't difficult given how beautiful she was.

Nanny loved to bake pies. She would have dinner ready for my grandmother and grandfather when they got home from work, and I usually helped her prepare the meal. About once a week, she baked pies, and she showed me how to make dough. She would make enough for her pies, and then she would give me a small ball of dough to play with. Yet rather than play, I used the dough for my own recipes, with Nanny assisting me.

When she had some extra money, Nanny would take me to Hammond's, a candy store in downtown Denver. They had the best candy, and I loved the smell of their store, which was also where they made the candy. My Nanny could drive, but it was more fun to take the bus because it was an adventure. We'd sometimes make our way to an inner-city lake named Sloan's, where Nanny and I would walk and feed the ducks with old bread that she had saved just for our walks.

On Saturday nights, I loved being at her house and sitting with her on the couch to watch *The Lawrence Welk Show.* My Nanny looked just like all the blue-haired ladies that appeared on the show, only she was more beautiful. We both loved listening to the orchestra play a waltz or a polka, and we loved watching all the beautiful women, like the Lennon Sisters, sing to the camera. I remember thinking how all the men in the orchestra, all with Brylcreem in their hair, sure were handsome. Only later did I learn what a sponsor was or what Geritol did. It was, indeed, "Won-da-ful, won-da-ful," as Lawrence would say.

My Nanny and I would play sometimes and sometimes we'd just sit, and I'd watch while she did her chores. At an early age, I learned from my Nanny the value of touch. She instinctively knew that touching someone in a nonsexual way could heal many wounds. Her fingers worked magic every time they came in contact with my skin. Even before I knew what massage was, she would rub me down and literally soothe away my worries, making me feel good all over.

This had a huge impact on me. Whereas my family was not affectionate, my Nanny saw the benefit of massage and wanted me to see it, too. I'd lie on her lap as she massaged me all over with one of her hand lotions. It was great.

One time, an adult in my life asked me who my best friend was. They probably expected me to name another kid in the neighborhood or my brother, but for me no one was a better friend than my Nanny, not even my mother.

Those afternoons with Nanny came to an abrupt end when I started school. Every child dreads the first day of school, and I was no different. When my mother dropped me off, I couldn't stop crying. I knew she wasn't abandoning me, but I just didn't want to spend the day without her, Nanny, Grandma, or someone I could trust. Those women were my guardians and protectors. I feared what I might have to endure in a world that did not care for me as much as they did.

By age six, it was pretty obvious I wasn't like other boys. I was introverted, afraid, insecure. I know many gay men who grew up feeling very alone and afraid of the world. I was one of those boys. I probably felt that way just because I knew I was different.

Gender roles are present from the day we are born, and by the time I was old enough to figure out that I was supposed to be like my father and my older brother, I panicked. I knew I was more like my mother. She laughed more. She enjoyed life more. She genuinely cared about everyone. Ever since I can remember, I gravitated toward my mother.

Somehow I knew that I was a mama's boy and that that was not good, but I wondered why it was bad. Why should I have

have to go out and make friends when I have my mother? She was a real adult who cared about me. Somewhere around age seven, I decided that my new best friend was my mother and not my Nanny.

I had dolls when I was a child. Surprise. My favorite was a talking Casper the Friendly Ghost doll. It was made out of terry cloth and had a plastic face. When you pulled the string, it would say things like, "Hi, I'm Casper," "Will you play with me?" or "Don't be afraid."

I'm not sure what my mom thought of my attachment to that doll, but she never tried to take it from me. Instead, she let me play with it and take it with me on the ride to school, though I had to leave it in the car when I got out. "Boys don't play with dolls," she told me once as I started crying for my doll. She apologized, and I could see the concern in her face. I was supposed to make friends at school, but instead I was becoming more attached to her and Casper.

There was this local children's television show in Denver called *Fred 'n' Fae*. It was just like *Romper Room* or *Captain Kangaroo*, and it aired every weekday afternoon, just in time for children to watch it when they got home from school. During the show, they always showed cartoons of Casper or Popeye or something else that was popular. When I heard that kids could be guests, I told my mother that I wanted to go on the show.

I had to hound her several times before she finally sent a letter to the television station. Sure enough, in a few weeks time, I got a response, and I was sure my television career was about to take off. I thanked my mom and told her she was the best mother and the best friend in the whole world.

During one of my two appearances on the show, I was chosen by Fae to pick one of six special squares that they had on a wall. Behind each square was the name of the cartoon that was to be shown next. I pressed the button underneath a square, and down dropped a slide to reveal Casper the Friendly Ghost, and then the cartoon started. My mother sat off camera as I basked in my newfound television celebrity. She was clearly excited by all the magic that television could produce in the early 1960s. During commercial breaks, I'd wave to her, and she'd wave back.

I didn't hate school, but after school I preferred to run home to Mom rather than go play at someone's house. I would tell people that my mother was my new best friend. I got to know my grandmother Allene, who was a bookkeeper for a linen supply company that serviced restaurants throughout Colorado. Occasionally, my grandmother had to work in Glenwood Springs, a small mountain town about a three-hour drive west of Denver, where her company's other plant was. She couldn't just drive there in the morning and come back in the afternoon like you can today, so she would stay at a hotel at one of the natural hot springs in the Rocky Mountains. Once in awhile, my parents would allow me to take the train up to Glenwood Springs to see her, and she would let me play all day at the hot springs while she worked. When her work was done, she would drive me back to Denver.

My grandfather Vernon worked in a typewriter repair shop, and sometimes he would take me to his shop and let me hang out with him. He was a master at fixing broken keyboards and rollers, and when he could, he would let me play with typewriters that were so broken, it didn't matter if I messed them up. But I wasn't much for play. I wanted instead to learn how to type, and when I did play, I pretended that I was a secretary at his office. My grandfather didn't seem to mind. I remember the smell of all those inks and cleaning chemicals where he worked. All those fumes probably contributed to his death, but to me, they smelled wonderful.

All my relatives were hardworking, proud people. Other than my mother, none of them talked much. They didn't seem to be hiding anything, but there was just a sense that personal lives should be kept private and that loud talk was improper. For example, they all knew about my Nanny's past life, but they never condemned it or commented on it. They probably all knew that I was gay, but they didn't wish to say anything about that either. My cue was not to say anything unless I had to, and I never had to.

My mother was always involved in civic activities. She appreciated having me help her. One night we'd be making centerpieces for an upcoming bowling banquet, the next, it might be bags for a Halloween party. I was a good worker, and the fact that I was doing it for her made it even more important to me.

Back in the 1960s, people ironed everything, including underwear. My mother, like a lot of women, had a laundry and ironing day, and you can imagine all the clothes that came from three boys and a police-officer husband. Rather than try to do it all herself, she turned laundry day and ironing night, which was usually Friday, into a business opportunity for me. While I was at school, she washed, but then at night, she'd pay me three cents for every handkerchief I ironed, five cents for every shirt, and ten cents per bed sheet. I could easily make a couple of dollars every Friday, and for a kid back then that was a lot of money.

We would watch TV while we ironed. My favorite show on Friday nights was *The Man from U.N.C.L.E.* While we worked, my mother and I would talk about everything you can imagine. She'd tell me about her girlfriends or what was going on in the bowling leagues. I didn't have much I wanted to share, so normally I'd just listen or make up some small talk. These moments with my mother were priceless.

Dad used to work evenings. Because the bowling league met on Saturday mornings, Mom and I would sometimes work into the night on league stuff. There were always score sheets to tabulate, matches to determine, or some other paperwork that needed to be done. Then we'd take a break and drive down to the A&W to get a root beer float.

Over time, our close relationship grew, even though we rarely talked about anything serious. On Saturday mornings my mother worked at the bowling alley, and I was right there beside her. We'd leave the house around eight o'clock, and she would buy me breakfast at the snack bar. There were dozens of youth bowling leagues, and she kept track of them all, with a little help from some other mothers and me. It was a lot of work, but she seemed to enjoy it. I admired her dedication, her willingness to see things through. Being together made the work fun for both of us. Her friends would say things like, "I wish I had a son like Mike," which made us both happy.

Come Saturday afternoon, she'd be back home doing her chores while I sat at the kitchen table and played cards or worked on updating the bowling books. While she worked, she'd talk on the phone. She'd spend hours talking to her girlfriends or to her mother. Mostly they gossiped but not in a mean way. She'd lock the front screen door, and caught up in a call, she'd forget that she had locked people out. My father would have to bang like hell to get her attention. The telephone was her way to stay connected with the world. I never once took offense that she was talking with her friends and not with me.

My mother liked to look good, and my job as her friend and pseudodaughter was to help her. Sometimes that was a challenge because her weight fluctuated. When she would get down to a slender dress size, she'd want to get all dolled up and go somewhere to show off her new figure. But even when she was heavy, she didn't hide herself. If I couldn't put her into a slinky gown, I'd dress her in a blouse with a silky collarless shirt underneath and a nice pair of slacks. Since she was heavy more often than skinny, she usually wore pants, in black or in other dark colors, with an elastic waistband.

I also learned how to do her hair, as well as my grandmother Allene's and my Nanny's. It required rollers, Dippity-Do, aerosol hairspray, and plenty of time under our portable, hooded hair dryer, so I didn't do it often, but when I did, boy, did they love it. My mother liked to wear her hair big, so when she had an updo with a hairpiece on top of that, the total effect could be awesome.

In the basement, we had a great space with a bar that was perfect for parties. My parents would hold parties for the bowling people, the city government people, and everyone and anyone in the neighborhood. They liked to make sure everyone had a good time. I would help out by picking up dirty dishes or serving cocktails and snacks. Sometimes I would play bartender, and I loved that job. It allowed me to be with the adults. Even as I turned thirteen, I still had no desire to be with other kids my age.

When I couldn't be with my parents, I had no one else I could spend time with, so I spent many a Saturday and Sunday holed up in my bedroom. I had a television set in my room, which was not common back then. I could watch black-and-white TV all day, and I loved watching westerns.

Audie Murphy was my favorite cowboy. I would fantasize about being him. I liked the action.

I would also fantasize about being kidnapped. I would lie on my bed and imagine myself walking down Colfax Avenue, strolling among all the people I was told to avoid. There I am, acting coy, when suddenly a good-looking older man opens a car door and shoves me inside. I scream for help, but it's no use. Cars were big back then, so inside the car on this huge backseat, the man pulls down his pants, then he pulls down my pants, and as I see the street lights pass above me, we connect. It wasn't a terror fantasy—it was a sexual fantasy. A couple of times, I did go walking on Colfax without my parent's knowledge, but no one approached me and nothing happened.

My mom used to tell her friends how clean my room was. It was because her vacuum cleaner, a Filter Queen, was always in my room. I used it for cleaning, sure, but I also used the long hose for, well, entertainment.

My mother never opened my door and barged in. She would knock and would come in only if I said it was okay. She was very respectful that way. When she came in, she would ask, "Is everything okay?" and I would say yes, and that would be the end of it. Despite all the time I spent with her, I just couldn't tell her how different I felt from other kids. I knew her limitations.

Then one day the thing we never talked about came up anyway. I was fourteen at the time. At the end of a school day I came home to find a letter I had written laying on the dining room table and my mom sitting there beside it, looking at me. I had written this very homoerotic letter to a teacher and then felt too shy to send it to him. But the things I said in it were so real to me that I didn't want to throw the letter away either. I thought maybe I'd find the courage to send it one day, so I hid it behind one of the pennants pinned to my wall. As my mom was straightening up that day, a pin fell out of the wall, and the pennant and letter fell right into my mother's hands.

"That's not a very nice letter," my mom said, looking at me. I was getting ready for a big lecture about the evils of homosexuality, but to my surprise, she said nothing more. She didn't even confiscate the letter. I was so embarrassed, I ran to my room and stayed in it until the next day.

That was the one and only time my mother and I even came close to discussing my homosexuality.

Christmas was the most wonderful time of the year at our house. Long before there were lavish contests for home decorating, my parents spent months building and preparing their outdoor Christmas display. My father would start building figurines in October. He had an amazing talent for figuring out a scene and then constructing the parts to make it come alive.

One time my father was making a wooden elf in the garage, where he kept all his tools. He tried to teach me some basics about woodworking and other manly things, and I was happy to assist him. I would stand there and hold the board while he drew an outline and measured it. Once we were done, I couldn't wait to run inside and help Mom cook or bake or whatever she was doing.

As Christmas approached, my mother and I spent hours wrapping Christmas presents, not just for our family, but for local toy drives and other projects she was involved in. We'd also do a lot of holiday baking, and I can tell you, there is nothing like making cookies and desserts with your mother during the holidays.

By the age of fifteen, I had completely taken to the art of outdoor holiday displays, and I had two of the best teachers in the state. One year, I even won the Edgewater city contest. When the local paper interviewed me, I made sure to thank my mother, father, grandmother, grandfather, great–grand-mother, and everyone else I could name.

I probably stood out more than others because everybody knew my father was Sergeant Jones. Sometimes I could get away with things that other kids couldn't; other times it seemed that I couldn't get away with anything. Sometimes my father would try to make it seem that the advantages out-weighed the disadvantages, like when he would confiscate firecrackers from kids, then turn around and give them to me. I would turn around and sell them to make a quick couple of bucks.

A few times our car windows were bashed in, and we knew immediately that it was because my father was the long arm of the law in Edgewater. It was a part of life that we just accepted. He spent most of his career working with juveniles, or youth programs, and was the kind of cop who was not out to get anyone. He worked a lot with first offenders, hoping to get them off the track they were heading down. Sometimes kids would get picked up for shoplifting or other petty crimes. If he busted you, he was more likely to let you go and tell your parents than take you down to the station or write a ticket. He also had the option of letting kids perform community service, a decision that was entirely at his discretion. He'd have them cutting weeds or sweeping floors. It was all per-fectly legal. Back then, it was easier for an officer to use his own good judgment.

When your father is a police officer, there is always a tension woven into your life, and you learn to accept it. We knew quite well that every day he went out, there was a possibility he would not come home. That's just how it is in law enforcement families.

One time my father responded to a disturbance call at a local drug store, which had closed for the day. It was nighttime, and the caller said he heard banging and other noises coming from behind the store. My father was the only officer on duty. He thought someone was probably drunk and had fallen near the drug store.

As he approached the store, he drove around back but noticed nothing. He then drove around to the front of the store and saw a car parked at the front entrance. As he got out of his squad car, he noticed a man hiding underneath the car. My father drew his weapon and ordered the man out from under the car. The man underneath the car had a gun, which my father quickly secured.

Dad then wisely ordered backup from Denver Police. They were there in minutes, and when they entered the drug store, they came across two men who had broken in. After shaking those two down, weapons were found on each of them.

The men were arrested and my father was all right, but the incident did shake him to his core. He didn't tell us about what had happened until much later in life. If I had heard stories—true stories—like that as a kid, I would have been a wreck. By the time he retired in 1983, he had risen to Assistant Chief of Police.

When I turned sixteen, I wanted to get my driver's license just like every other kid. I didn't want to drive so I could go cruising, however. I wanted to drive so I could take my mother out to do things.

Since we both loved theater, we went to a lot of small play-houses. Comedy shows, more than dramas, were our favorite because they gave us the chance to laugh out loud together. I got to see something other than my bedroom walls, and she got to go out and have a good time.

My parents didn't push me to start dating girls. Their approach was mostly hands-off, and that gave me freedom to explore what I wanted. They taught me how to be a decent and respectful person, and that has really served me well. They never asked me who I was dating or when I was getting married.

Still, I decided that maybe it was time I got out and tried to make friends, though I didn't know how to go about it. I tried to date in high school, but it was a disaster. I was afraid to ask girls out, so they would have to ask me out. But I got the feel-ing that girls asked me out because they felt sorry for me. By this point, I was already a weight-lifting champ, but I was still an outcast and a loner.

My sexual being, however, was blossoming just as I was becoming successful in bodybuilding. During my junior year, I had sex with a teacher. During class, I could tell he was inter-ested by the way he looked at me. At an early age, I had developed gaydar, or a gay sexual radar, that made me sensi-tive to something in men's eyes. I could see when they were interested in playing.

"Mike, I can help you with your studies, if you like," he told me. Back then, flirting and intimacy between teachers and students was common, but no one talked about it. Since I really was struggling with my grades, I said yes and hoped he would just happen to do it in the nude.

I went to his house many times. If his very attractive wife was there, he would simply say he was tutoring me. But when she was gone, we got naked and had fun. He was a good-looking man in his late thirties. Because of his help, I not only got laid, but my grades went from a D to a B in his class.

After graduation, my looks started to mature and got better. My body was looking great from all the weight lifting. I started wearing contacts instead of glasses, and my acne problem started to dissipate somewhat. I was very happy with my entry into adulthood, but I had no idea that I would be able to take those looks all the way to the bank.

My mother was still the best friend I had. She needed to share her life in a way she couldn't with her husband or her two other sons. And I needed a friend, plain and simple. My duty to my mom was to be there always to listen. She would vent with me as if I were a woman, and I understood her frustration from a woman's point of view. If she had any legal or financial questions, she'd come to me first. Maybe she saw me as the ideal child, embodying the good qualities of both a son and a daughter.

It always seemed I was the one all the women in the family could talk to. I remember Grandmother Jones, who lived to be ninety-six, told me that she always felt like a fifth wheel around the family. "When you are around, you always make me feel welcome," she once told me. "You give me more attention than anyone else."

I have always been able to recognize when someone is lonely, maybe because I know the feeling all too well. I am quick to react and give that person the time and attention they deserve. It's my nature, I guess.

My Grandma Jones gave me one bit of advice: always stay on your toes. This advice has served me very well on many occasions. One that I remember in particular involved a well-dressed businessman I arranged to meet in a hotel room.

"C'mon in, buddy!" the businessman said when he opened the door. "How are you? Can I get you anything?"

I can't tell you why, but suddenly my gut turned into knots. "May I use your bathroom?" I asked.

"Sure." He took a seat at the table in the room where he had his laptop up and running.

I went into the bathroom and looked around. There were no toiletries. No shaving cream. No razor. No deodorant. No toothbrush. All the towels were still very fresh and folded. It looked like the maid had literally just cleaned the sinks.

"When did you get into town?" I asked from the bathroom, running the water but not doing anything with it.

"Yesterday," he replied. "Boy, I sure can't wait to have some hot man-on-man action."

I stopped cold. His words sounded very odd, as though he were reading my ad word for word.

I shut off the water, dabbed my hands on a small towel, and carefully walked out of the bathroom. Once I stepped into the foyer of the hotel room, I was prepared for just about anything. "This sure is a nice place," I said, which was a huge lie, because it looked just like every other Hilton or Sheraton I'd been in. I used that line as an excuse to look around the room.

As I looked in the closet, what few hairs I hadn't shaved off my back were standing straight up. There were no clothes and no suitcases. I wanted to ask, "Travel light?" but I decided not to do that. It was pretty clear to me what it meant when someone has been in a hotel room for a day and there are no suitcases, clothes, or toiletries in the room.

I gazed around the room a bit more. "Everything okay?" the handsome businessman in the tie and dress slacks asked.

"How did you hear about me?"

"From your ad."

That was all the confirmation I needed. "I'm sorry, I gotta go," I said. "I'm really not feeling well. Sorry 'bout that."

He immediately stood up and walked toward me, prompting me to walk backward toward the door. I was expecting him to say something like, "Why are you leaving so soon?" or "Can I make you feel better?" But he didn't say a word other than "okay" in a very matter-of-fact tone. No emotion, no trying to change my mind. Nothing, just like his toiletries.

"Nice to meet you," I said, my heart racing faster than my feet. I closed the door to the room behind me and walked briskly down the hall. I pushed the down button several times. I got in, hit the L button, and held my breath until I got to the busy lobby.

Was that a setup I had just walked away from? The nice clothes and no suitcases probably meant that he was a cop and this was a sting, and at any moment a reporter would pop out of the closet with a camera. There was no way to know, so I listened to my gut and left. Thankfully, I hadn't gotten undressed.

CHAPTER 5

MY THIRD YEAR WITH ART

◨

For awhile, I had a personal training business and, in the 1990s, my own small gym. Some of my clients were serious about getting in shape and some were not. Inevitably, many of them came to hit me up for sex, even though I made it very clear that my personal training business was strictly about weight training and fitness. After three years of owning the gym, I was burned-out. After all, I had been a trainer for twenty years. Plus, the rent was going up dramatically, so I decided to shut it down. Some of my personal training clients became escorting clients. Some continued to see me just for fitness training at other gyms. Some saw me just for massage.

My massage and personal training services were never a cover for my escorting services. I enjoyed doing all three because it allowed me to focus on the needs—whatever they might be—of my clients. When I advertised, it wasn't always clear what services I offered. One ad proclaimed, "Best Personal Trainer, Readers Choice, 1997 and 2000." Then the name of my business, Mike Jones Body Masters, appeared followed by, "see also ad under massage." In my ads, I wore next to nothing.

As in any other industry, there is a spoken code in the massage business. "Do you provide happy endings?" When a caller asked that, I knew they weren't talking about Swedish or deep tissue massage.

"What kind of massage do you give?" the curious would ask.
"What are you looking for?" I'd asked.

"Full body." That was code for sex or a massage of "every-thing" on the body. "Does it come with release?" That's code for ejaculation.

"Yes, I can do that." Then I'd schedule a time and place with the understanding that it's two hundred dollars an hour at my place, three hundred dollars and up per hour at any other location or on short notice. There may be an additional charge for parking and other expenses. "Should I bring my massage table?" That was another question I would ask to confirm that the client knew I was providing "other" services.

I wouldn't work in rooms that were accessible from the street, so motels were out. When United Airlines had a large number of employees based in Denver, it seemed like every pilot and flight attendant with a layover had my number. And when national touring companies for Broadway shows came through town, I did a lot of massage business, most of it being strictly massage, some of it being "other" services.

Art was a client who got the benefit of my skill in massage, personal training, and escorting. "How can I get muscles like you?" he asked one summer afternoon. He clearly had no intention of working out to the point where his biceps became noticeable. Still, I showed him how to do biceps curls and chest exercises. I had a weight bench and a set of adjustable dumbbells in my living room. Wearing just a jockstrap, I lay on the bench and pumped out a few bench presses for him.

Art's eyes were wide with excitement. He wasn't watching my form or asking about the weight. He was focused on my pecs, watching with awe as they flexed.

"Do you want to try it?" I asked.

Straddling the bench, Art tried doing some bicep curls. I made sure he used only twenty pounds, and even with that weight, he struggled.

Many clients love when I suddenly hit the ground to knock out some push-ups. While Art was doing curls, I did a set of twenty push-ups. I then encouraged Art to try it. He struggled with those, too, having to use his knees for balance on the floor.

"You'll get the hang of it," I told him, slapping him on the shoulder blade. For kicks, I did some sit-ups while I had him hold my feet. He seemed to enjoy when I pulled my chest into his face. Seeing his erection, I took him to the massage room for our usual routine.

After two years, I often felt as though Art and I were still on a first date, and it was a blind date to boot. I knew very little about him, and that was a bit unusual. After a few years, I usually know my clients pretty well. They learn they can trust me and that they don't need to be as careful as they were when they first met me. This enables them to open up.

Art played his cards pretty close to the vest. I knew he was married and that he rode a motorcycle, but that's about all I knew for sure. I had figured out that he lived in Colorado Springs and that he probably worked for a church there. And I knew he really liked sex toys and methamphetamine. Other than that, he was a mystery.

But keep in mind, Art was a client, first and foremost. He was entitled to a lot of privacy. That was part of our unspoken agreement. I didn't ask and he didn't tell. As long as I got paid, things were fine.

The next time he came, he was ready to burst. "I am so ready to go!" Art told me, rushing into the massage room. Within seconds, he was undressed and called for me to come in right away. Maybe he had to be somewhere shortly.

"Jack me off now!" he said. Standing completely naked, he was very hard and very excited. I placed him on his back on the massage table and started stroking him. His body was so stimulated that I feared he would go into convulsions. Within minutes, the magic was over. "Wow," I said before he could. "That was quick."

His panting was heavy as he lay there in an intense afterglow. Five minutes later he was reaching for my crotch and fondling it madly. A few more minutes of intense rubbing, and he was hard again. I grabbed his dick and soon he ejaculated again.

"You stud!" I told him, slapping his butt. I put a hand towel on his groin, but this time, rather than scurry off to the bathroom, he lay there for a few minutes. I stood by his side as he rubbed my torso and midsection.

"You know, Mike," he said softly, "I really like coming to see you." He kept rubbing my body, wearing a smile that showed how good he felt.

"Thank you."

When he was ready, he sat up and cupped the towel over his groin. I stood back to give him some room, but to my surprise, he pulled me in closer. He did not want to hug me, but rather to touch me some more. After about a minute of that, he gathered his clothes and went to the bathroom.

"Let's watch some more porn."

"What would you like to see?"

"How about something raunchy?"

I put a XXX movie called *Intensity* into the DVD player. Art sat on the couch, fully clothed as usual, watching every movement of the action on the television screen. The men in the video were hairy and muscular with short, cropped hair. Art seemed to respond well to these performers, who were in their thirties or forties and called each other "Daddy." He would get hard, but he would never take off his jeans or unzip them. When he got to a certain point mentally, he would go into the massage room and take off his clothes.

Once we were done, he lay there blissfully. "You know, Mike," he said, "I always look forward to seeing you. You really make me feel good." That may not sound like much, but coming from Art, it spoke volumes. After two years, he was beginning to feel a lot more comfortable being intimate with me. Maybe it was the meth or maybe it was the length of time he had known me.

"Thank you," I said as I combed his hair back with my fingers.

We spent several sessions just sitting and watching porn. He was no longer interested in vanilla porn, where the actors get naked, touch each other, giggle, and then jack each other off. He wanted the sleazy, butt slapping, butt fucking, down and dirty, "lick my boots" kind of man sex—but only as an observer. I arranged another show for him featuring Matt and me playing with each other. He loved it and again paid extra. I was starting to feel like I was charging him too much just for sitting there and playing with himself.

Each time, he had a new toy or accessory in his little canvas bag. He'd pull it out, try to play with it, screw it up, and then I'd have to instruct him on its proper use. Since he was so green, I took my time with him. With someone like Art, you had to explain everything.

Before I entered the massage room, I'd hear the sounds of items being scattered about. I'd walk in, and there would be Art, naked among the new toys he just bought. Sometimes he'd have them sprawled on the massage table, and sometimes they would be on the floor.

"Show me how this works," he asked, pulling out a device known as a penis pump.

I showed him how to put lube around the open end of the cylinder so that when he slipped it over his penis, it created suction against his skin.

"Oh, that feels good," he exclaimed. I put my hand on the cylinder while he pumped it up. His eyes were open with excitement over this new adventure.

Once he tired of the toy, he hopped onto the massage table and stretched out on his back, waiting for me to perform my magic. Within minutes, it was all over. He didn't scurry off anymore and would sometimes stare into my eyes with a look of deep affection.

I became increasingly concerned about the infatuation I saw in his eyes. Was he falling in love? I tried not to think about it. I had had to tell clients I couldn't see them anymore because they had crossed an emotional line that I did not feel comfortable with. Art was too good a client to lose through such unfortunate circumstances.

"Mike, have you ever ridden a motorcycle?" he once asked.

"Your motorcycle is important to you," I commented.

"Yes, it is," he replied, still feeling me up and down.

"I have ridden one a couple of times but just in a parking lot. I've never taken one out on the road."

"I remember you said you had some friends die in motorcycle accidents." Art smiled as his mind wandered. "You shouldn't let that scare you. I can teach you how to ride safely."

"Sure," I said, even though I would have been surprised had he been willing to go out with me in public.

Without saying anything more, he got up, grabbed his clothes, and went to the bathroom.

I always imagined guys who rode hogs as being Hells

Angels types who were large, unkempt, wore leather or Levi's, and were totally unconcerned about the world around them. Art wasn't anything like that. In fact, he was just the opposite. Motorcycles are hugely popular among the forty and over crowd, so Art was probably merely reflecting that trend.

One day he came out of the bathroom, ready for a chat. "Do you ever get tired of being an escort?" he asked casually.

"Yes. It can be very unpredictable."

"What do you mean?"

I tried to come up with a brief explanation. "Most of my clients don't book in advance, only when they are ready. I can't just go to dinner or a movie, especially at night because that's when most men call. And it's tough to go on vacation, because if I don't work, I don't get paid."

For some reason, Art didn't respond. He gave me my money and showed himself out the door. Maybe I had given him more information than he wanted.

I knew Art would ask about anal sex at some point, and sure enough, he wanted to try it during our next session. I agreed. When the day arrived, I could tell Art was nervous, so I tried to reassure him.

"You don't have to do this," I told him.

"No, I want to," he told me, and I believe he did want to try it, but he was clearly unnerved by the thought.

I again explained how we would do it.

I then slipped on a condom and lay on the massage table on my back. Art touched me, rubbing me all over, before he climbed on top of me. He was very tense, so I massaged his chest and legs as he tried to sit on top of me. The first few attempts did not go well. He just wasn't relaxing enough.

"Let me know when you want to stop," I told him, bracing him with my hands.

Art kept trying, but he just too tense. I lay there, letting him have full control of the situation.

"How are you doing?" I asked.

"It hurts."

"Do you want to keep trying?"

"Oh, yeah. I really want to do this." Without pushing, I guided Art down toward the table again. Once I was in place, I instructed him to breathe with deep breaths, almost as though he were panting. That would make it a lot easier to take.

"How are you doing?"

Art opened his eyes, took a breath, and then seemed to relax a bit. As he got more comfortable, he tried to take a little bit more but couldn't.

"We can stay just like this," I told him, my hands on his thighs.

Art wanted to go further but was frustrated. "I've always wanted to try this. I'm sorry, Mike."

"Trust is the key," I told him. We stayed as we were for a few minutes more, me lying on my back while he sat over me. His legs were tingling, so he got up, and we continued our session as usual.

As he left, those big sad eyes were peering deep inside my soul. "I feel like we made a connection," he told me.

"As long as you liked it, that's all that matters," I said.

He gave me my two hundred dollars, hugged me, and walked away, motorcycle helmet in hand. He seemed more ashamed than usual, much like he did when he first came to see me. For many men, being penetrated is the ultimate sign that you are a homosexual. Perhaps a dick up his ass was more than he could handle.

"Do you have any brothers, Mike?"

Just as straight guys fantasize about having sex with a roomful of sisters, gay guys sometimes fantasize about doing a roomful of brothers.

"I have two, one older and one younger."

"Are they as good looking as you?" Art asked.

"In their own way," I replied.

"Are they hung like you?"

I laughed. "I really wouldn't know. We're not that close." I put some more lotion on a dry spot I noticed on his thigh.

Then he asked me, "Do you have any kids?"

"No." I knew he had children, but I did not want to go there with him, so I didn't say anything.

"Have you ever wanted to have kids?"

I sighed, thinking of my mother and her three children. "Not really. I don't have a problem with children, but I can't say I ever wanted to be a father."

Art's breathing picked up a bit. "Kids are great."

"Wow," I commented. "I'll bet you're a terrific father."

He looked me in the eyes. "You mean that, don't you?"

I nodded. "You're a kind, gentle man. Your family is lucky to have you."

Art really lit up on that comment. What struck me as curious was that he was in a happy mood. Rather than enjoy a moment of intimacy with another man and then be brought down by the reality of family life, it was almost as if he were seeing it all work together wonderfully. Now that was something I was curious about.

"I'm a very lucky man," he said.

"Congratulations," I replied. "You deserve it."

When my mother got sick, I racked up a ton of debt flying back and forth to see her. Sometimes I bought the ticket on the day of the flight at a high price. Like I told Art, if I wasn't working, I wasn't getting paid, so when I would be gone for a week or longer, there was no money coming in. I was living paycheck to paycheck, or client to client, during 2005 and working extra hard when I was home.

The beauty of being an escort is that with just a smile and the right touch in the right place, you can be as distracted as you like and still do your job. Art was enjoying our session, but my mind was still in Las Vegas with my mom. All I could think about was that she was lying in bed in pain.

"Have you ever thought about doing anything else with your life?" Art asked as he lay there after his release. *Why is he asking me this? Is he trying to save me?* I had to stop and bring my mind back to Colorado. I asked him to repeat his question, which he did. Without thinking, I gave him an honest answer.

"I'm sorry, Art, I'm not really focused on this right now." I hated saying that because he might want to know more so he could comfort me and show me how much he cared about me. "My mother is very ill. As you can imagine, I'm a bit distracted."

Art rubbed my arm. "I'm sorry, Mike," he offered. Yet rather than pry any further, he got up, grabbed his clothes, and went to the bathroom.

I was grateful he didn't inquire further. Perhaps he didn't want to know about my personal life or my feelings. Maybe it's true that intimacy among most men can only go so far. If true, that's sad, but in the escorting business, it can be a plus. No one gets too involved, which means no one has to stray too far from his comfort zone. I wanted to stay snuggly within mine, as did Art. It was the deal we made more than two years earlier.

A woman called to ask me if I would do massages at a bachelorette party. I said I would need to think about it. I'm not a prude, and women clients had made use of my services before. It's just that I wasn't sure I needed the money badly enough to do an entire bachelorette party.

The next day, I called her back and told her that for a total of four hours the price would be two thousand dollars plus expenses. I pulled that price out of the air in hopes of discouraging her. To my surprise, she said fine and nailed down the date, time, and place. I admit I was a little nervous, but with two grand I could pay a lot of bills. And it was for only four hours of work. I figured any man on the planet would have jumped at the opportunity.

I arrived at the Westin Hotel and went to the suite number she gave me carrying my massage table and other assorted accessories. She had me set up my table in one suite and don my costume in another. At first I thought she wanted me to dance a little for everyone. I had my shorts, shirt, and music all set to go. Then at the last minute she told me to go into the massage room to receive the girls one at a time. That was no problem for me. I kept hoping that she wouldn't try to haggle with me on price.

A young woman in some sort of sleepwear came in. I had set up the room with candles and scented oils, and I was wearing boxers when she came into the room. After her, the others came in one by one. They were all under thirty. Only one woman asked me to keep my shorts on. Most of them were pretty liquored up. Hey, it was a party.

I spent about fifteen minutes with each woman. Some would strip only to their underwear. A few came in and wasted no time taking it all off as I stood right in front of them. It wasn't turning me on, but I wasn't sure what I would be asked to do, so I had brought along some Viagra just in case.

Just like my male clients, most of the women that night just wanted to be touched sensually. I massaged their face, back, shoulders, and legs, and if they desired, I would massage their breasts, buttocks, and their groin area. I think some of them may have had orgasms, and some made interesting sounds, moving their bodies in curious ways.

"Can I put it in my mouth?" a couple of the women asked. "Whatever you want, baby." I didn't know for sure, but calling a woman "baby" in that setting seemed to work well. Again, it did nothing for me, but they seemed to enjoy it.

One woman went even further. "Give it to me, Daddy," she moaned. It was odd for me to hear that from a woman. But since it was my job that night, I gave it to her, even though I wasn't very hard, and it didn't go in very far. I of course used a condom, because I *always* practice safe sex.

Come midnight, I had completed my service. Talk about feeling like a stud. My contact paid me and off I went. I also collected several hundred dollars in tips from the women, so all in all I had one of my most profitable nights ever.

The July 2005 attacks on London's subway system and a double-decker bus, in which fifty-two people died, made a big impression on me.

Innocent people were killed because of differences in religious beliefs, so I started questioning the role of religion. As in politics, there are extremists. People claiming to have the Truth on their side can be the most dangerous of all.

Since I suspected that Art worked for a church in Colorado Springs, I wanted to ask him about his religious beliefs and his background. If he did work for a church, I wondered what their policies or feelings were regarding homosexuality. There is no shortage of preachers and religious leaders who have taken joy in skewering homosexuals. It raised a lot of money for them, but I never understood why they had to be so vicious and so absurd.

For example, Jerry Falwell said this about the September 11th tragedies on the television program *The 700 Club* two days after the attacks:

> I really believe that the pagans, and the abortionists, and the feminists, and the gays and the lesbians who are actively trying to make that an alternative lifestyle, the ACLU, People for the American Way—all of them who have tried to secularize America—I point the finger in their face and say "You helped this happen."

This coming from a man who told the world that a little cartoon character named Tinky Winky from the television program the *Teletubbies* was a homo because he has a triangle on his head and he carries a purse.

"What's next, polygamy? . . . Why not? And why not bestiality?" Falwell told CNN's Wolf Blitzer in 2004. It was enough to make me scream.

Maybe the reason all this was coming up now was because of my mom's illness. The problem I have with organized religion getting mixed up in politics is connected with something my mom taught me long ago—that my relationship with God is personal. That proved to be true for me. I have found religion to be far more effective when it isn't crammed down my throat.

I've always had a problem with comments from leaders of organized religious groups who feel the need to force their beliefs on everyone else. They make comments, then deny making them, and all the while it's apparent they think a lot more about gay sex than I do.

According to mediamatters.org, Falwell has a history of denying his own inflammatory remarks regarding homosexuality. In 1984, Falwell publicly denied having verbally attacked a gay community church until a videotape surfaced showing Falwell calling members of the church "brute beasts" and "part of a vile and satanic system [that] will one day be utterly annihilated." The Associated Press reported that story on September 25, 1985. When Falwell was ordered to pay five thousand dollars to a former pastor of the church, he responded, "This situation is only one more example of harassment by a militant homosexual group."

The fact that people like Falwell use religion and spirituality to justify such comments is what angers me most. To say that God loves you but only if you are heterosexual goes against any kind of true Christian feeling.

In 2004, Pat Robertson called lesbians and gays "self-absorbed hedonists . . . [who] want to impose their particular sexuality on the rest of America." Based on the fact that around 15 percent of my clientele worked in a church or for an organized religion, that's hardly what I'd call *us* imposing our beliefs on *them*. Basically, they seem to be able to find gay sex wherever it may be—and to take advantage of it.

All that fire and brimstone coming from the mouths of the homophobics makes me angry. I suppose what really concerns me is how one of the world's oldest and largest religions feels free to call me a whore while its followers have no problem taking advantage of my services.

I've heard it said that anywhere from 30 to 50 percent of Roman Catholic priests are gay. Friends of mine who grew up Catholic or are priests will tell you the percentage is much higher. Yet rather than embrace the gift of sexuality that these men bring, the Vatican sees fit to view these men as evil and undesirable.

That's the definition of hypocrisy. When you have people like Jimmy Swaggart and Jim Bakker getting dethroned for preaching one thing and doing something different in the dark, that's hypocrisy. Nothing makes me more upset than people of faith who support church policies against homosexuals and other alleged sinners and who have *themselves* acted on homosexual feelings of their own.

In 2005 the Vatican put out a paper called *Instruction Concerning the Criteria for the Discernment of Vocations with Regard to Persons with Homosexual Tendencies in View of Their Admission to the Seminary and to Holy Orders.* Wow, that's a mouthful. Basically, here is what it has to say about queers: "Regarding [homosexual] *acts* . . . Sacred Scripture presents them as grave sins. The Tradition has constantly considered them as intrinsically immoral and contrary to the natural law. Consequently, under no circumstance can they be approved." So are they talking about the homosexual act of cocksucking or interior decorating?

The document goes on to say that, "[We] believe it necessary to state clearly that the Church, while profoundly respecting the persons in question, cannot admit to the seminary or to holy orders those who practise homosexuality, present deep-seated homosexual tendencies or support the so-called 'gay culture.'" By gay culture, are they talking about *Queer Eye* and disco?

Cardinal Adam Maida of Detroit helped further explain the Vatican's position when he commented on the sex-abuse accusations against Catholic priests. "It's not truly a pedophilia-type problem but a homosexual-type problem," he said in 2002.

Or to Cardinal Francis George of Chicago, who at the time wanted to make a distinction between a man who sexually abuses boys and one who sexually abuses girls. Referring to John Geoghan, a former Boston priest accused of abusing more than one hundred children over a thirty-four-year period, George said, "There is a difference between a moral monster like Geoghan . . . and someone who, perhaps under the influence of alcohol, engages in an action with a seventeen- or sixteen-year-old young woman who returns his affection."

I understand wanting to serve the Lord. Such devotion can give meaning to one's life, especially when you have a positive impact on the lives of others. Anyone who is willing to make such a sacrifice should be given all the tools possible for success. Forcing people into the closet and calling it the Lord's will is wrong.

I admire the truly brave ones who come out of the closet and admit that they are gay but still desire to serve to humanity. Unfortunately, the Catholic Church and most other churches have made it impossible for people who are honest about themselves to live a life dedicated to their fellow humans.

About five years ago, I got a phone call from a gentleman named Jack visiting from a neighboring midwestern state. He told me he was on the faculty of the Department of Religious Studies at a university in his home state. It may or may not have been true, but I did notice that my caller ID showed he was calling from a university in that state. He told me he was married with a family and yet wanted to have intimacy with another man.

During our first meeting, I could sense his hesitancy with the sexual act. He felt guilty, and he was uncomfortable. The more he saw me over time, the more comfortable he felt, and he appreciated the fact that I would listen to him, even when he wanted to talk about religion, and that I would let him pray if that was what he wanted to do. In fact, he was so grateful that he sent me a package containing spiritual books that he asked me to read. Enclosed was also a card:

> *Mike, Thanks much for the time together talking about life. I appreciate your vulnerability and honesty. Thanks also for accepting me and listening to me even though I am a "born-again" Christian. Enclosed is the book I was talking about. Read it with an open heart . . . be careful and don't be too critical . . . Thanks. Hey, thanks also for your courage to let me pray. I know that wasn't easy. Next time I am in Denver, I'll give you a call and we can meet up. Jack*

One time we were talking about religion after he had achieved release. Since it was a subject he enjoyed, I figured it was okay.

"Are there some sins that are more extreme than others?" I asked.

"A sin is a sin is a sin," he told me as he lay naked on my table. "It doesn't matter if you are a homosexual or a mass murderer."

"There is no distinction?"

"No, there is not."

You can imagine what I was thinking. Here's this hypocrite rubbing my ass while his wife is at home with his kids, telling me that I am no better than a mass murderer. I said nothing more.

Most of our sessions, however, were not as intense on the verbal side. Sometimes we talked about religion and sometimes we'd just get naked. Mostly, he wanted to hold me and talk to me, and sometimes he wanted something raunchier. His prayers went something like this: "Dear Lord, thank you for letting me be with Mike and thank you for letting us share our time together. Please let Mike have a happy life, let him be complete."

How the hell did I start attracting men who wanted to pray instead of jack off?

By the end of 2005, I was starting to tire of being an escort. I had been one my entire adult life, and while the money was good, I was feeling burned-out. Like most jobs, you can only do it for so long before you have to make a change. I pulled many of my ads and started telling clients that I was going to close the business.

Art had scheduled another afternoon appointment, and he was on my list of clients to inform that I would no longer be taking appointments. I performed our usual routine, wanting to make sure he achieved release because that would make him feel better. As he lay with a towel over his penis, I figured that was the best time to tell him.

"I'm not going to be an escort anymore," I told him, trying to get the words out as fast as I could.

Art sat up quickly. "What?"

"I am, for lack of a better word, going out of business."

"But you can't!"

I grabbed his hand and tried to calm him.

"Would you consider seeing just your current clients like me?" he asked anxiously.

"Art, I can't . . ."

"Please, then, just see me, okay?"

Wow, he sounded desperate. I couldn't have predicted that he would be so upset over my decision.

"I can't, Art."

"Please, Mike." He then grabbed his wallet from his pants and pulled out three—not two—hundred-dollar bills. "Please, Mike, I need to keep seeing you."

I winced and took the money.

"Art, you don't understand . . ."

"Please, Mike, for me?"

I sighed heavily. "Let me think about it, okay?"

"Okay, that's good." Cupping his nakedness with his left hand, he made his way to the bathroom, closing the door behind him. He came back into the massage room and put on his clothes right in front of me. "Thanks, Mike, you're a good man," he said as he put on his shoes.

On the way out the door, he gave me another big hug. "Please, for me, okay?" he said, putting his finger to my lips as if to quiet me.

As he walked down the hall, he did so walking backward, looking at me as though his train were leaving and it were the last time he might see me.

I was feeling uncomfortable about how Art had reacted to my announcement. No one gets as nervous as he did unless there are deep feelings involved. He had clearly fallen for me, perhaps not in an obvious romantic way, but he was infatuated. That happens a lot with clients who see me for several years. We may meet just once a month, but our session involves feelings that come from their core.

That night, I couldn't get Art out of my mind. His eyes followed me wherever I went. As I looked back on our last year, I realized that Art had "the look." It was there in his eyes the whole time, and I was only now seeing it. His eyes would follow my every move in the massage room. At our first sessions, he used to avoid looking right at me. Now he couldn't take his eyes off me.

Crap. All those conversations about escorting and brothers and motorcycles! He was in love with me. I was sure of it. The final proof was how desperate he was to keep seeing me, at all costs.

God, was I tired. *Of everything.* My mother was going to have surgery out in Las Vegas, and I didn't have a good feeling about it. In fact, I wasn't getting a good feeling about anything.

I suddenly saw Art as a storm that was brewing. He had fallen for me, and it appeared that he wasn't going to leave me alone. Ever.

> *Someone told me long ago*
> *There's a calm before the storm*
> *I know, it's been comin' for some time*

John Fogerty, writing back in his Creedence Clearwater Revival days, had gotten the words just right for the feelings that haunted me.

Then I thought that maybe I was wrong. Maybe Art just wanted to keep seeing me because he felt he could trust me. He knew I wouldn't fall in love with him, and that gave him the safe distance he needed to explore his sexual frontiers without really having to confront his homosexuality. Maybe all he wanted to do was play around and be my buddy.

How confusing. The main reason I wanted to keep seeing Art was because he was a good customer who paid what he owed and required little maintenance. It wasn't like I had to work all that hard to keep him happy.

CHAPTER 6

MY MOTHER'S DEATH

⊞

By 2003, when I first started seeing Art, my mom's calls to me almost always ended in tears. She and my dad had moved to Las Vegas in 1993, and at first she had loved her new life, working at the Golden Nugget Casino, making new friends wherever she went. But she started having stomach pain a few years later, and the doctors never figured out what was wrong with her, not until almost the very end. Meanwhile, both her parents, who'd moved to Vegas when she did, died in 2000. After that, her pain kept getting worse. I gave her as much comfort as I could over the phone. She would say she loved me, and I would say I loved her. She never told me much about her fears, and I never told her much about mine.

Just about the time Art started using meth before every visit, my parents flew back to Denver for my niece's high school graduation. My mother was in pain, but it was tolerable. Mom and Dad spent a few nights with me that visit. One evening we were at my dining room table playing cards when, all of a sudden, she doubled over. The pain was sharp and terrifying, but the incident was short. We wanted to take her to the emergency room, but she refused. Within an hour, she was still in pain, but she was back to normal.

When she returned to Las Vegas, her pain grew worse. Her appetite was dwindling. Some days, she wouldn't eat a thing.

We all knew there was a big problem when my mother did not feel like eating.

She kept going back to the doctor. He would run tests, but they would all come back negative. It was probably just an infection, they told her over and over again. They would send her home with some pain pills and told her not to go to work for a few days.

"Mikey, I'm in so much pain," she would cry over the phone. "They don't know what's wrong with me!"

All I could do was tell her that everything would be fine and that she had to keep pressing the doctors for more tests and more information. One time, I finished a call with her just as Art was showing up for a session. It was about that time that I began praying. I was in midprayer when Art and his big smile greeted me at my door.

One afternoon just before the arrival of a client, I got a call from my younger brother, Terry. Mom had been taken to the emergency room with stomach pain and other problems. He gave me some of the details but did not indicate that I needed to fly out to Vegas right away. I asked him to keep me posted. As you can imagine, I couldn't stop thinking about her.

A few days later, Terry called me again, this time to tell me that Mom needed surgery. Then he told me to prepare myself for what he was going to say next. I took a seat on the couch. The doctors had learned that the blockage Mom had was actually "a cancerous tumor."

I wasn't surprised. It made perfect sense that her pain all these years was caused by something as strong and serious as cancer. Finally learning the truth hit me right in the gut, as hard as if someone had punched me in the stomach.

By this point, my mother had already been in the hospital

for a week. I told my brother I'd be in Vegas as quickly as I could. I cancelled all the appointments I had for the next few days. For those clients I couldn't reach, I left a recording on my voice mail explaining that I would be out of town due to a family emergency.

I can't believe it, I said to myself over and over on the plane. Cancer is such an ugly word. No matter how prepared you think you are, it still hits you like a train. Mom was always blessed with good health. Her mother lived to be eighty-six and her grandmother, my Nanny, lived to be eighty-seven. Cancer was in our bloodline, but it was odd that it would show up in my mother while she was still in her sixties.

I said a prayer on the plane. I wasn't praying to anyone or anything in particular. I was just praying, praying for a miracle. It was odd, to say the least. I started wondering what my life would be like without my mother. That was even odder.

Two surgeries were performed on my mother that time, one on her colon and the other on her bladder. They removed what they could, but the doctors told us they were unsure if they'd gotten all the cancer.

I hated seeing her curled up in a fetal position, shaking with fear and pain. She was shell-shocked. I couldn't do anything for her. Now it seemed that no one could do anything for her. She was heavily medicated, but that may have given us more peace than it gave her.

"Get some sleep," I whispered to her, stroking her brittle hair.

She kept trying to stay awake to enjoy every moment she could. I knew she wanted to get up and walk. In fact, she wanted to get up and walk out of the hospital. The sedatives were strong, however, so after a few hours of fighting the medication, she ultimately relented and fell asleep. Other than chemotheraphy, there was little that could be done, we were told. Holding her hand and being with her was apparently all I could do. After a few more days in the hospital, Dad and I took her home.

"Did you hear the one about . . . ?"

The next time I saw her was a few months later. I was pleased to see Mom try to laugh again. She struggled through to the punch line of a simple joke. It was difficult to watch. But at least she was trying. Maybe the chemo pills were working. Maybe my prayers were being answered.

She had to get her blood drawn every other week. The pain seemed to be increasing. I admired her ability to smile through it all. She still had her fighting spirit. I kept wishing and hoping and praying that she would beat the cancer.

Six months later we got a heartbreaking call from Mom's oncologist. It was Christmas 2004, and I was in Vegas with my parents. The doctor's words are still vivid in my mind: "The pills are not working, and the cancer is advancing." She would have to start intravenous chemotherapy.

My mother and I sat and cried while Dad waited in the hall. We just couldn't understand. She looked like she was doing better. She felt better, sort of. Intensive chemotherapy would leave her frail and weak, and there was no guarantee that it would halt the cancer's spread. I might have tried to talk her out of the heavy-duty chemo, but by that point she'd had enough talk. She needed some positive reinforcement, so I gave her as much of that as I could.

All this was especially hard for my father. The man who barely showed any emotion suddenly found himself overflowing with emotion. I feared it would kill him, but to the contrary, it helped release what he had been bottling up his whole life. Now he would cry and not be ashamed of it. How ironic. My mother's illness strengthened him. Suddenly, my father is telling me every day how much he loves me and how proud he is of me. That was great, but it pissed me off as well. Why did it take a tragedy like this to knock him out of his self-imposed straitjacket?

I spent a few more days with my folks and then flew back to Denver for New Year's Eve, though I did nothing but stay home and cry over my mother. She called me a few days later to tell me that she and Dad had decided to move to California. Several years earlier, my brother Terry had moved to southern California to get married. Given how intense Mom's new chemotherapy would be, they felt they should be closer to family.

"Whatever you do, I will support you," I told her over the phone. I liked that they would be closer to Terry, but I feared the stress another move would cause. It was too late, though. They were already preparing to be in California by the end of January 2005.

I flew to California every other month. Each time, she was noticeably weaker and thinner. She still had a strong spirit, though. When I visited, she couldn't wait to put on some makeup, grab her purse, and go somewhere. Sometimes she could handle an entire afternoon out and about. Sometimes she'd make it to the car but be too sick to leave the driveway. I was spending time with her and that made me feel good. When she was awake, we talked and laughed. I'd fix her hair or give her a massage. I spent a lot of money that year on travel, and it was all worth it.

In October 2005, we all took a day trip to one of the local Indian casinos. It wasn't Vegas and the Golden Nugget, but we hoped it would bring her back to life. All the loud bells, flashing lights, and the smell of winning in the air would make her come alive. We got her a hotel room just in case she needed to rest.

I had been praying more and more throughout the year, and my prayers were becoming less free spirited and more traditional. As my brother was checking in for us, Mom and I waited in the hotel lobby. I told Mom I would be right back and stepped just a few yards away from her.

Dear Lord, I love my mom so very much, please let her have some enjoyment today. Please let her win something so I can see a smile on her face again. Amen.

I wanted badly to see some joy on her face, but I felt so helpless by that point. I've never been religious, but watching my mother deteriorate had rekindled my spiritual side. I found myself praying for a miracle.

You could tell she was struggling to walk. Carefully placing one foot in front of the other as I held her by her arm, she smiled as she approached an open seat at a table. The seats at these tables are high, and it took us a minute to get her into the chair. With all the strength she could muster, she got in without my having to lift her up. She quickly placed her bet so she could be included in the next hand. I stood behind her with my hand on her shoulder as I watched her play.

Three-card poker is just like the five-card variety, only with two fewer cards. You can get a flush, a straight, a straight flush, a pair with a high card, or, ideally, three of a kind. The game moves a little faster, too. Mom was aglow, the first time I'd seen her so animated in more than a year.

Her style was to look at only one card at a time. Sometimes she wouldn't look at any of the other two cards. On one memorable hand, the first card she drew was a king. That was good enough for her. She did not look at the other two cards, but indicated to the dealer that she was still in the game by putting her chips on the cards that were facedown.

Next, it was time for the dealer to turn up the player's hands. Talk about a minor miracle. Mom had three kings, and that made her bet worth about $450. At that moment, I felt that my prayer had been answered. She got very excited. She was smiling and laughing, and you could see the life come back to her entire body. I was so happy I started crying.

Yet after a couple of minutes, she started having pain in her stomach again. The grief on her face was plain to see. She wanted to keep playing, but she just couldn't. "Mikey, I'm tired," she said. "Can we go to the room so I can rest a bit?"

We took our time getting to the room, taking each step carefully. She was still holding on to her winning chips. Once inside, she inched her way to the bed and collapsed on it. She wanted to sleep but couldn't. The look on her face said that she feared not waking up. I sat by her and held her hand. She asked me to turn on the television for her. Every huckster in Southern California seemed to be on, each one selling something you couldn't be without. She'd closed her eyes but never really fall asleep. Looking closely at my mom's face, I could see the change. Her youth was gone. There was no vibrancy. I wasn't sure what was left, if anything.

Before long, she sat up, full of energy again. "Mike, we sure as hell can't win any money up here in this room." So back down to the casino we went. We played poker for a few more hours but didn't hit any more winning hands. As she played, I could see how tired she was getting, but she did not want to give in to it. "It's okay, Mom," I told her. "Let's go home. We'll come back another day." She held on to my arm as we walked out to the car.

My mind was racing during the drive home. My mom was

too quiet. She was giving up. Once home, she went directly to bed. By now, Mom lay in bed 98 percent of the day, sleeping at times and crying at times but rarely resting. As she lay there, I watched her for a bit before I turned the lights out. Then it was time for me to leave, but first I booked a ticket for my next visit in early January.

Shortly after Christmas, however, my dad called to say I should probably come back to California sooner. He said she was getting visibly worse. The doctors were talking about hospice care. He didn't know what to do. Could I please come out and help with things?

When I arrived, I saw for myself how much worse my mom had gotten. My dad also looked terrible, his face showing his distress and confusion. I spent the next week with them at their apartment. When possible, I let my mother fall asleep in my arms. Now that she was just skin and bones, I could pick her up a lot easier. Just like anyone else, she needed to be touched—now more than ever.

She looked like a zombie. You could read on her face each morning how long and harrowing the night before had been. Her fear that once she fell asleep she wouldn't wake up was growing. Every hour, she would start crying, and then I would start crying. I could do little more than hold her and tell her I loved her and that everything would be all right. I kept praying, but I was losing faith fast.

"Do you remember the first time you tried to use a video camera?" I asked her. "Or how about the time we tried to figure out that recipe from the *Galloping Gourmet*?" These memories made me smile but did nothing for her. Was she awake or was she asleep? At that point, I realized I no longer envisioned her regaining her health.

I extended my hands and massaged my mother's face. My

Nanny told me that a good massage is not only immensely helpful to the person being massaged, but it also tells the masseur much about that person. Gently rubbing her forehead, cheeks, and nose, I could vividly feel her pain. I know that sounds corny, but the muscles in her face told me plainly how much pain she was in. She yearned to be touched, so I continued to rub her face lightly. She responded well to it. That allowed her body to relax and trust me. Within the hour, she was asleep. It was one of my few moments of joy that entire season.

Growing up in the 1960s, I got a sanitized version of death and dying, sometimes in black and white but never in blood red. People died and that just seemed to be the end of it.

Her bones almost came through her skin. I feared that the slightest amount of pressure might snap one of them. Age spots and discoloration covered most of her once-beautiful skin. As I rubbed her abdomen, I could almost feel her organs starting to shut down.

"Do you remember the surprise anniversary party that Russ, Terry, and I threw for you and Dad?" I asked her. "You always liked it when I bought you a corsage, didn't you?" I could almost see her smile, or so I imagined.

Once again, I massaged her face.

"Please take care of my family," she mumbled.

I had to sit back and take a breath. In her final days, she was so concerned that those she loved would face horrors without her around. She was calling out to anyone who might hear her, asking them to take care of her family. Or maybe she hadn't really spoken, maybe it was her face calling out only to me, or maybe it was my imagination. I fought back tears, just as I had been doing for more than a year.

"I love you, Mom. You're a queen."

Every hour or so, she would come to life with amazing clarity, only to end up crying again. She'd try to say something, but I couldn't understand her. I guess at that point, even I wasn't taking her words seriously. I just wanted her to be at peace, but she kept crying.

"What's wrong?" I asked her.

The fear in her eyes scared me. I held her hand and tried to assure her that everything would be fine. Of course, I knew it wasn't going to be fine. And then I would start crying.

"Am . . . I . . . dying . . . Mike?" she managed to ask.

"Everything will be fine, Mom." The truth was that I wasn't ready to admit that she was, indeed, dying.

"Please don't make me go!" she would exclaim in a moment of clarity, clutching my hand with all her strength.

"Mom, you're not going anywhere." I would put my hand on her forehead and try to massage her back into a state of rest.

Around January 7, hospice personnel sat down with my dad, Terry, and I and explained how to prepare for her death. "Here's the best way to administer morphine," I remember someone saying. I wanted to ask him if some morphine could also be administered to me.

The first time I placed the liquid morphine under her tongue, my mother shook her head and tried to spit it out. She was angry, but that was good because it meant she was fighting. Instead, just as the doctor had suggested, I hid the morphine in some applesauce and spoon fed it to her.

My mother did not want me to see her in the condition she was in. Likewise, I hated her seeing me so drained and depressed. I had not worked out in weeks; all I was eating was soup and crackers. I appreciated the break I got when the home health-care assistant came by to give her a sponge bath.

Yet at the same time I feared falling asleep and having my mother pass without me beside her.

I reached a point where constantly hearing my mother cry and listening to her confusion about what was happening became too much to bear. Without thinking, I finally did what I had hoped to avoid doing. I put my mouth to her ear and whispered, "Mom, you're dying."

To my surprise, her tears suddenly stopped.

I waited a few moments. "Do you understand what I just told you?"

She took her time but eventually nodded. After that, I swear she never cried again.

A nurse had been at our house almost twenty-four hours straight. She said my mother was not in pain and that when the process of expiration began, it would last about two hours because her body would shut down rather quickly. But two hours turned into eight. Crying right in front of my mother, I waited. Twelve hours after the beginning of the end, even the nurse said she was amazed that my mother was hanging on for so long.

At two in the morning on January 9, she finally passed. Dad, Terry, his wife, Mona, and I were there with her. In her final hour, we were all so exhausted we could barely stand. There we were, with our mother for one last time before the mortuary came to take her away forever. I wanted to go with her.

On the day of my mom's funeral, we placed a few meaningful items in her casket before closing it. Dad brought a ceramic angel and my brother, a deck of cards. I took the queen of hearts from a regular deck and wrote, "You will always be twenty-one to me. Love, Mike." The reference to a winning blackjack hand was the best I could think of at the time. I know she appreciated it.

There were almost one hundred people at the service. My sister-in-law's entire family had been with us throughout the last few months. Even one of Mom's former co-workers from Las Vegas made the drive to come say good-bye. That meant the world to me.

I cried the entire service. My mother and my best friend were gone. What would I do now? When the Minister asked if anyone had anything to say, I immediately stood and said this:

> Mom, what a beautiful person you were. Everyone that came into contact with you loved you. You always wanted to make people happy without asking for anything in return. Oh, how you loved your grandchildren. You simply did not have enough time to do all the things a grandma should do. You will always be the blackjack and the three-card poker queen.

At the cemetery, her grave is on top of a hill overlooking a valley. As they lowered her into the ground, we threw flowers on top of her. And then I stopped crying. I simply stopped. Maybe I was too exhausted to know what was happening—or what was about to happen. I thought of my favorite line from *Les Misérables*: "To love another person is to see the face of God," and it seemed so right.

My life returned to what passed for normal for me. As I returned home and tried to start a routine, I found it very difficult. I knew I needed to book appointments to bring some money in, but I had no motivation. Then my first new client ended up being more than I bargained for.

A man named Mark called me from a phone number with a 719 area code to book an appointment. He looked like he was in his midforties and had blue eyes and very dark brown hair. He was a little taller than me and very polite. He was an attractive man. I guessed that he was in the military.

I showed him to the massage room and told him he could get undressed in there.

He took one look at the room, however, and shook his head. "This isn't going to work," he said. I was miffed, as I really didn't have much else to offer. "Can we just lie on the floor in the living room?"

"Let me put something on the floor," I offered, going to the closet for a sheet to put over the carpet. I also grabbed a couple of pillows and set everything up like a makeshift bed. I turned out the lights and lit a few candles, placing them throughout the living room.

"That's great," Mark said, taking off his clothes as he stood by the couch. I took off my shorts and lay down on the sheet. Mark lay down next to me. "Just hold me, okay?" he asked.

I was fine with that, so I simply placed him in my arms and rubbed his body lightly. There was no talking and, to be honest, nothing was happening.

After about twenty minutes, however, I could feel teardrops falling on my chest. "What's wrong?" I asked him.

Mark buried his face deeper into my chest. "You don't want to hear about it."

I pulled him in tighter. "Try me."

Mark took in a deep breath. "I'm dying," he said rather calmly.

In my entire escorting experience, that was the first time I had a client say those words to me so bluntly. "What do you mean, Mark?" I asked.

In words broken up with tears, Mark confided that he had a rare form of leukemia. "Do you know what leukemia is, Mike?"

I wasn't sure of the exact definition, but I nodded and said yes.

"I am very upset. I really needed to be held by another man tonight."

"I'm so sorry, Mark," I told him. "I don't know what to say."

"You don't have to say anything. I'm sorry for bringing my problems to you."

"Everything will be okay," I whispered. I don't know why I said that.

I grabbed another sheet and pulled it over us. "Tell me about it," I said, snuggling my face to his. "I want to know."

Fighting back tears, Mark told me about his illness. After he was first diagnosed, he went online to do as much research as he could. In the process, he found numerous other people in cyberspace who were suffering from the same disease. He developed online friendships with several of them. He was speaking with such intensity, I wondered if this was the first time he had ever confided in anyone about this.

All seemed to be going well for him until he'd logged onto his computer that morning and learned that one of his online friends had died. "It was more than I could take," Mark cried. "That's when I called you."

For the next half hour, we lay there in silence. We had gone past one hour, but that night, I didn't care. I wanted to do as much as I could for this guy. "Do you have anyone you can talk to?"

"My wife."

Not a surprise because I had noticed his wedding ring.

"I know I am here with you, but I really do love her. She'll have to face such a huge responsibility by herself when I'm gone." And he kept crying, softly.

I stared up at the ceiling, trying not to get caught up in his grief. "What responsibility might that be?"

Mark sighed and buried his head in my chest again. "I have three children."

As far as I'm concerned, you can't hear a story like that and not be touched. He lay in my arms silently for almost another two hours before he decided it was time to get dressed and leave. He told me that he and his wife had not had sex since his diagnosis. That didn't surprise me. The slightest bit of stress can kill your sex drive. During our visit, we did not have sex either, and he seemed okay with that.

"Thank you for listening, Mike," he told me. Dressed and ready to go back to his life, he handed me two hundred dollars plus a little extra.

I thought about Mark over the next few weeks. If I was watching the news and there was a story about a new cancer treatment, I would think of him. If I saw someone in the military, I would think of him. If I simply saw a good-looking man, I would think of him. Mark had touched me, and I hoped it wasn't because I pitied him.

I wasn't sure he would call me again, but out of the blue he contacted me to schedule another appointment. I was so happy to hear from him.

When he came again, we lay on a sheet in the living room just as we had before. This time we had sex but nothing hot or heavy. Afterward, he told me two more of his online friends had died. I let him lie in my arms again for more than an hour.

"How are your children?" I asked.

That question really made Mark light up. He told me about

all the projects they were doing at school, how their dance classes were going, a recent sleepover they hosted, and all the activities in which they were involved. He talked about all this while resting his head on my chest.

Then, like lightning, he was up and said he had to be on his way. He thanked me again and told me what a wonderful time he had had.

I saw him two more times before he disappeared from my life. Both times we enjoyed intimacy, but on his last visit, he told me how he and his family were going to the Mayo Clinic to see if there was anything they could do for him. He sounded hopeful, but I could tell that he was nervous.

I never saw Mark again. He may have beaten the leukemia or he may have died. The time we shared may have helped him get through the worst time of his life. I gave Mark comfort, just like I comforted hundreds of men before him.

CHAPTER 7

DISCOVERING TED HAGGARD

⊡

After almost two weeks of going from the bathroom to the couch to the kitchen to the couch, with few if any stops in between, I had to do something. One afternoon, I couldn't take my own stench anymore, so I got up and showered. Then I put on what few clean clothes I could find and went outside for a walk. It felt good, but I could only do it for an hour. Back home, I plopped down on the couch again, but at least I'd gotten out and done something. Everything in moderation, including moderation.

I started doing a little more each day. During one particular burst of energy, I went into my closets and started throwing things out. Just as my father and I had done a few weeks earlier when we'd gone through Mom's belongings, I wanted to get rid of whatever I no longer needed. Old papers. Old clothes. Most of my trophies from bowling or bodybuilding competitions. They just didn't mean anything to me anymore.

From California, I'd carried home my mom's collection of porcelain and glass angels. I created a little display in her honor on a desk in my bedroom, where I placed all the angels and some of her jewelry and perfume bottles. It wasn't meant to be a shrine but a reminder that she is here with me, in spirit.

"Please help me go forward from here," I'd pray aloud to her. "I don't know what's going to happen, so please stay close."

I called my father twice a day. I was merely checking in, so we didn't talk much. Phone calls aren't like real visits, where you can touch someone or look into their eyes. My father assured me that he was fine and said that I didn't need to check up on him so often. I cut back on the calls, but to this day I talk with him two or three times a week.

Come the end of January, I had just enough money in the bank to pay February bills. Calls were coming in for massage appointments. I still had ads out there, so it was good to be getting calls. As a masseur, I can almost meditate while I'm giving a massage. Both parties benefit.

I also started getting modeling calls from an art school where I'd modeled before and from individual artists and artist groups as well. I even had a few weight-training clients call me to get started again. Those were great, too, because the workouts took place at the client's home on their own private equipment, making it very focused on them and their training issues and at the same time providing me with the perfect escape from my issues.

I had stopped actively advertising escort services in favor of massage and personal training. Occasionally an old client would call, but I was trying to limit the escort side as much as possible and was, for the most part, succeeding. I simply didn't have the strength to be "on" for those clients. I did, however, find that I had enough energy to play tennis again and enjoy the early spring sun, and I tried to focus on those positive things.

My friend John Kite, a piano player at the famous Brown Palace Hotel, invited me to come to the hotel and join their weekly sing-along in the bar. I hadn't done that in months, so I went, and it was nice to have people hug me and tell me how sorry they were to hear about my mother. My friend Lloyd Peltzer invited me to spend a few days with him in the moun-

tains relaxing and playing cards. I did that, too. It was good
to be out again. After the trauma of my mother's death, I realized how short life really is, and I became determined to use
the time I have well.

Valentine's Day was hard. I had always sent my mother a
card, candy, or flowers. Her birthday and Mother's Day
were only a few months away. I tried to prepare myself on
the assumption that getting through those days would be a
struggle.

I still had days when all I could do was sit on the couch and
cry. What was I going to do with my life? I was forty-eight, I
didn't have a partner, I was tired of escorting and tired of massage, I wasn't close to my brothers . . .

I was still hoping I would meet someone. I did meet a man
on one of the gay sex lines, but as you can imagine, it went
nowhere. The sex was boring and the one thing I needed—
intimacy through touching—wasn't something he could
provide. How ironic that I had spent my entire adult life
touching other people, but when it came to my own desire to
be touched, I went begging.

Art came to see me two or three times during this period. The
first time he came to see me in 2006, he asked me how I was.
Since I had already told him about my mother being ill, I confirmed that she had finally passed.

Art showed some emotion but not a lot. "I'm sorry," he
said.

I smiled and tried to think about the hour's work ahead of
me.

"What did she die of?" Art asked.

I told him. He smiled, gave me a hug, and off he went to
take off his clothes.

I wasn't expecting anything more from him. He was paying two hundred dollars for a good time, so he was entitled to a good time. I took a breath, went into the massage room, and began to entertain him.

I'd turn forty-nine in May.

Have you ever heard a voice that sounded familiar, but you just couldn't place it?

I've always been intrigued with history, and in 2006, like most of the nation, I was swept up in *Da Vinci Code* mania. I love a good mystery. I was never much of a reader, so documentaries like those aired on the History Channel are gems for me.

I was on my couch sometime in April watching a documentary on the Antichrist. I didn't know what to make of the concept, but I was fascinated by how it had been kept alive for thousands of years.

I can rarely sit still for an entire hour of television, though, even when I'm intrigued. So a few minutes into the show I turned up the volume and started straightening up around the apartment. I also had the blinds and the door to my balcony open, since there was wonderful, early summer, Rocky Mountain weather that day.

"Every generation thinks it's going to be the last one," the television blared in the background. The speaker went on to talk about big churches, so I admit I was more focused on the papers I was filing.

Then I thought, *Boy, that voice sounds familiar.* I went back to the couch to watch, but the man I'd heard speaking was no longer on. As I continued cleaning, I heard how, throughout history, people have expressed the need for hell and punishment, and how the Antichrist has served as the perfect figure for attracting all evil so it doesn't infect others.

I was looking for a particular receipt when that familiar voice started speaking again. I couldn't tell you why this voice intrigued me. I remember thinking that there was nothing spectacular about the voice. It was kind of mousy, actually. In fact, it sounded kind of gay. *Maybe he was someone I knew,* I thought briefly, *or maybe he had been a former client.*

I continued shuffling through my receipts and doing other things while the moderator and his interviewees spoke about the human spirit and how it drives people to do what they do. After giving up my search for the missing receipt, I took a break and lay on the couch, watching the last thirty minutes of the documentary.

As I watched, that voice came on again, and now I could see his face. Front and center sat a man in a collared blue shirt and tie sitting before a library of books. I sat up and leaned in closer to the television so I could see the screen.

"Oh, my God!" I shouted. "That's Art!" By the time I recognized him, his name had disappeared from the TV screen. But I could hear his voice—and see that trademark smile of his.

"Wow," I said to myself. I had thought Art was connected with a church of some sort, but since I saw books in the background, I figured that maybe he was a professor of religious studies at some university down in the Springs. That would make sense. Too bad it was my policy never to ask clients about their personal lives. I'd have loved telling Art how I'd seen him on television and how good he looked.

I continued to clean once the documentary was over, but something wasn't settling right. I kept thinking about the show and about Art in particular. My curiosity was piqued. Why would Art be part of a documentary on the Antichrist, and why would he be on such an important show? I was curious as to what the connection was and decided to order myself a copy of the show.

As the day wore on, I kept thinking about Art. Thoughts of my mom and prayers to her still dominated, but now Art shared her stage. I did a little more paperwork, washed the evening dishes, and lay on the couch without crying that night, but I couldn't fall asleep until about midnight.

When I woke up the next day at my usual 4:15 a.m., I threw some water on my face, put some fresh clothes and a bottle of water in my gym bag, and headed out the door to the gym, stopping only for a quick cup of coffee. I started with half an hour on the treadmill. I've always found that doing some cardio before you lift weights makes for a good exercise routine, and that's what I have done almost every day of my life since I was a teenager. Exercising on a tread-mill is also a great way to wake up. Many people listen to music when they exercise, but I've never liked wearing headsets, so I normally listen to whatever is playing over-head. At the gym where I work out, there are several televisions facing rows of treadmills, stationary bikes, and other machines. They're all usually set on mute and tuned to different channels.

For some reason, Daystar, a religious network, was on one of the monitors directly in front of me. That was a bit unusual, since that's a channel you wouldn't usually see any-one watching in an inner-city gym. Lots of sports and soap operas, yes, but rarely overtly religious programming.

A full-figured woman with big brown hair talked directly into the camera. *She must be Joni*, I thought, since that name had flashed across the screen a minute earlier amid stylistic shots of clouds and people staring up to the heavens. Then a man appeared on screen, showing a lot of emotion and excitement as he spoke. He was wearing a blue collared shirt and had a big smile.

Oh, my God!

My eyes blinked with disbelief. There was Art on the screen again, less than twelve hours after I last saw him on television. *It couldn't be*, I thought. I had to stop and think. This was Daystar, not NBC or another big network. This was religious programming, and apparently Art is an expert on something religious. Besides, it was five in the morning. This had to be a rerun, and probably an old one.

Next, in a flash, his name appeared underneath his profile. I stopped the treadmill so I could focus on it. T-e-d. Hmm, his name isn't Art, but that's not a surprise. His name is Ted . . . H-a-g-g-a-r-d.

When I got home, I sat down at my computer and typed "Ted Haggard" in Google's search box. A second later, a slew of Web sites came up and listed prominently among them was www.tedhaggard.com. I double-clicked on the underlined phrase and up came the official Web site of Ted Haggard. Right in my face was Art's smiling portrait: clean-shaven with light brown hair and wearing a blue collared shirt with a white T-shirt underneath. He looked just as he did when he came to see me, just no motorcycle helmet.

I couldn't believe my eyes. Art is a reverend, and he has his own Web site and a lot of followers. Bouncing around his site, I found sermon after sermon, though I didn't feel comfortable enough to read any of them. The entire site was one big promotion for Ted. I clicked on a link to something called New Life Church. It sounded New Age to me, so I was a bit surprised to see just how Christian it was. There were so many places with references to Pastor Ted, "our" pastor and founder. Oh dear, not only is he a pastor, but this church is his handiwork.

My eyes grew wider the more I read. New Life Church was attracting some fourteen thousand members every year, according to the Web site. Then I came across something called the National Association of Evangelicals. I was not surprised that such an organization existed, but the number of members it claimed to have—30 million—caught me off guard. And Art was the president of this organization.

It was all too much for me to process in just one sitting. I got up to get some water but came right back to my desk to poke around some more. I thought of my last encounter with Art at my apartment, when he wanted to try out some new sex toys he had just purchased—and do meth. It also occurred to me that he knew my mother had just died and he had not offered to minister to me.

I've been around enough fundamentalists to know that they have very strong opinions of people who they deem sinners. These New Life people seemed pretty solid in their belief of what's right and what's wrong, so I could only imagine what they would think of me. And of Art.

I clicked on another link that my Google search had pulled up, but it was just a blog talking about how Ted Haggard is a jerk. Well, I figured, when you are that well known, someone's bound not to like you. I went back and forth between links, and soon a clearer picture began to emerge.

"This guy is huge," I said to myself. Again, I was just dumbfounded. Not sure what to make of any of it, I grabbed my wallet and some letters and walked out the door to run some errands. Now I was thinking constantly about a client who I honestly had thought little about before then. In a way, I thought it was cool—I love having celebrities as clients.

Around this time, Marilyn Musgrave, a representative from northern Colorado, was working on a proposal to amend the

U.S. Constitution so that "marriage in the United States shall consist only of the union of a man and a woman." We've all seen this before, and once again, Representative Musgrave from Fort Morgan, Colorado, felt that the entire free world would fall apart if two consenting adults other than a man and a woman had the legal right to get married. The more I read about her, the angrier I got.

"Neither this Constitution, nor the constitution of any State, shall be construed to require that marriage or the legal incidents thereof be conferred upon any union other than the union of a man and a woman," read House Joint Resolution 88, formally introduced in June 2006. It was a signature work of Musgrave's.

I hate when something like this gets used for political purposes. I wanted to write every member of Congress and tell them what hypocrites they were if they voted for this. Then I started thinking about Art and all the information I'd seen on his Web site. He hadn't called in over a month.

Sitting at my computer, I looked up www.tedhaggard.com again and also pulled up the Web site for New Life Church. *Let's write to Pastor Ted and see what he thinks about two men or two women having the right to marry.*

I sent an e-mail directly to Pastor Ted from an alternative email address, asking for his position on what Representative Musgrave was doing. "Do you support the efforts to rewrite the Constitution to ban gay marriage?" I asked. Sure, I could have worded it in a way to better conceal how I felt, but I was angry. And I had to know.

Two weeks later, I had not gotten a response. According to my e-mail records, I sent another message on May 18 and wrote, "This is my second request for a response. It really is not that hard. What is the church's and your position on the

Marriage Amendment currently before Congress? Support or not support? Thanks, Forest." Forest is my middle name.

Within less than two hours, I received a response from Ted Haggard's executive assistant, Meg Britton. At 2:04 p.m., she wrote, "Sorry, we've had some changes in our staff with the NAE (National Association of Evangelicals) who would normally answer your question. We are in support of this amendment. Thank you for asking. God Bless You."

That wasn't good enough for me. I had to know exactly what Pastor Ted thought, so I decided to write again, this time directly to him, to see if I could get a response to my question. This time, though, I added another pointed question: "What are your views on homosexuality?"

A few days later, on May 22, I received an e-mail from Pastor Joseph Winger: "Thank you for your inquiry about New Life Church. We do think that the Federal Marriage Amendment as endorsed by President Bush is a positive step for our nation. Regarding our view of homosexuality, we believe the Bible promotes marriage as a one man, one woman relationship. May God Bless You."

I sat there reading his response over and over. *How clever,* I thought. Winger didn't say that homos were going to hell, but clearly that's what he was suggesting. I wanted so much to think that Art's answer would be different, but why would it be? These were his spokespeople. I couldn't imagine that they would not be singing off the same song sheet.

My heart started pounding faster. All this time, this man had been coming to me every month to get naked and explore his homosexuality, and now I found out that he was one of the most powerful evangelicals in the world and that he wanted to keep people like me—and people like "Art"—from being treated fairly.

This was really pissing me off. I remember screaming at his picture on the computer. "You son of a bitch! How dare you!" Art and every straight-acting couple in America could get married and divorced as many times as they liked, yet two men or two women cannot get married even once, much less enjoy the legal benefits of marriage.

I thought of the many gay couples I knew. One had been together for fifty years. Yet, legally, my friends couldn't even enjoy second-class citizen status. I was becoming angrier by the minute. I was also becoming more nervous by the minute.

What if this constitutional amendment was ratified? What if more conservative Republicans got elected to Congress? What if someone like Art got a cabinet post?

As I sat in my apartment, I suddenly felt very alone. My anger started turning to frost. Few of even my closest friends knew that I was an escort, though I knew some of them must have seen my ads. No one in my family knew what I did. I remember thinking, *I need to do something about this, but . . . will anyone believe me?*

Not one to just sit around and let things fall apart, I grabbed a notebook and a pen. I figured, what the hell, I'll start writing down my options. "What do I do now that I know who he is?" I wrote in big black letters. "Do I not say anything and continue as always? Do I tell him that I know who he is? Do I go to his church and confront him in front of everyone?"

As I wrote, I started to shake. I ripped off that sheet of paper and started writing on a fresh one. My hands were trembling.

"Please don't let them take me," I could hear my mother saying to me.

"When you are around, you always make me feel welcome," my grandmother had told me.

"You're a nice kid, Jones."

"A sin is a sin is a sin."

"Do you have any friends?"

"Why are you still an escort?"

My tears were drowning me, just as they had back in January when I first returned home after Mom died. *Am I home? Is it all just a dream? Is there any chance I'm going to wake up to find that my mother and I are together at a casino in the winner's circle?*

I went to the couch to lie down. I was cold, which explains why I curled up in the fetal position. *Maybe if I just focus, my mom will come to me. She'll tell me what to do.* All the while, I kept seeing Pastor Ted's big smiling face from that photo on his Web site.

Could this be the hell they were talking about on the History Channel?

CHAPTER 8

MY AGONY

◫

Like most people, whenever I sit at my computer the first thing I do is check my messages. But after learning the truth about Art, my routine changed. Now I would open my Internet browser and go directly to www.tedhaggard.com, where I would spend hours searching.

The Web site, which has since been pulled, was nothing short of an Internet theme park dedicated to the man known affectionately as Pastor Ted. Everything you could think of was there. He came off looking very generous, even though many of his words were not.

I spent hours reading his sermons. One video clip I saw on www.beliefnet.com made me want to punch something: "People want to know, how do you have a good family? It is not hard. It is easy. First of all, you find a person of the opposite sex and then you make a life long commitment to them."

Ted was wearing a white shirt with a white T-shirt underneath in the video. I think he was wearing the same clothes when Matt and I performed for him.

"It is not hard [to have a good marriage]. If you lose your life for the sake of the one you're marrying, if you'll be faithful, and you'll be kind and you'll provide, then it will all work out."

But, gosh, Pastor Ted, what if I want to suck dick and my wife won't let me?

"If people want to be selfish, if people want to be greedy, if people want all their environment to be set up on their own terms, it really makes marriage and other relationships tough."

"Homosexual behavior is immoral," Ted had told Bill Moyers in 1993. "In other words, it's not the best, and that's not my opinion either." When pressed by Moyers to explain, Ted told him that "The Bible" was his authority on the subject.

As my head filled with his sanctimonious words, a migraine set in. It was apparent to me that I had now been given a new cross to bear, and his name was Ted Haggard.

There was also a part of me that just didn't want to believe any of it. Sure, it was all right there in front of me, but what if it was all nothing but a blogosphere conspiracy?

I spent the next several days tied to my computer. When I typed "Ted Haggard" into any search box, all kinds of items came up. I tried to look at as many of them as I could. In an article from the *Arizona Christian News*, Ted said the following:

> All of us were in sin. All of us needed redemption. If a person has homosexual tendencies . . . they need to practice abstinence just as a single heterosexual would need to practice abstinence. The difference would be that the single heterosexual could get married and become sexually active with their heterosexual partner, whereas the homosexual would have to practice spirit control and self-restraint throughout the balance of their lifetime.

Ted became president of the National Association of Evangelicals in March 2003, and came to see me a few months later. I tried to make something of that timing. *Now that he had power he could go out and get a call boy,* I thought. Or perhaps it was just a coincidence.

Ted Haggard talks to God while fasting in the Rockies.
God talks to Ted Haggard through a bowl of Cheerios.
Ted Haggard uses cooking oil to anoint highways.
Ted Haggard is a joke.
Marcus Haggard, Ted's father, was a pig farmer and faith healer.

"The percentage of people going to heaven and the percentage of people going to hell today is determined by how well you did your job yesterday," Ted told his followers once. *Is this guy for real?*

Ted also wrote several books, including *The Pursuit of the Good Life* and *From This Day Forward: Making Your Vows Last a Lifetime.* He even wrote a diet book, *The Jerusalem Diet,* in which he tells readers, "Don't let any substance determine how you live your day." I thought of all the meth Ted was doing. In another book called *Confident Parents, Exceptional Teens,* Ted wrote for a teenage audience on the importance of not lying.

I also spent hours at the New Life Church Web site. There was a trailer for a movie, *The Thorn.* It started off with some great visuals and orchestra music and talked about love, betrayal, sacrifice, and redemption; it was all about Jesus Christ and the story of his death. It took me awhile to figure out that the whole thing was a play, a passion play, produced by New Life Church.

I wanted so much to think that maybe Ted was just a frustrated theater lover. Then I found more homophobic stuff.

A long article featuring Ted appeared in the *New Republic* magazine in 1996. "It's Gay Pride week in Colorado Springs, as it turns out," reads the article. Ted is then quoted as saying, "I don't understand it . . . It would be like having Murderer's Pride Day."

Why would anyone say something like that? Is he saying that gay pride is the same as being proud of being a murderer? Is he equating us, as in "Art" and I, with the taking of human life? Was he just trying to be cute?

That comment really hurt me. I've been called a lot of names, but a murderer? I felt like I had been betrayed by a kiss.

A friend of mine said that no matter how old you are when you lose a parent, it leaves you feeling like an orphan. That's how I had been feeling since my mom died, and now I had to deal with my discovery about "Art," which was making me paranoid. I was feeling helpless. I needed to find something to do that would comfort me.

After my father retired, I wondered why he spent so much time sitting on the couch watching television. I wondered why he didn't go out more. You get nothing from sitting on your ass watching reruns and infomercials. It drove my mother nuts that my dad would rather stay at home watching the Hallmark Channel than go out to dinner. It drove me nuts, too. I saw him sinking into depression, and there was nothing I could do to help him.

And now here I was sitting on my couch watching daytime television. Sitting there with my remote, a large snack, and Judge Judy felt safe when feeling safe was what I wanted most. I began to understand my dad a little better.

One of my favorite TV shows of all time is *The Golden Girls*. The main characters—Blanche, Sophia, Rose, and Dorothy—are four mature women trying to get by and hopefully having fun and finding a little love in the process. Indeed, it is a show that appeals to women and gay men. Since I am gay and grew up as the daughter my mother never had, *The Golden Girls* has special appeal for me.

Sophia reminds me of Nanny, my great–grandmother. Dorothy reminds me of my grandmother, who was a very strong woman. I guess I'm the most like Blanche, even though the character was not a call girl, just easy. My mother would have to be Rose, then, which isn't exactly right. My mother was not ditzy like Rose, but she did have a sincerity and naïveté about her. My mother was a lot like Blanche, too, and in my opinion was every bit as beautiful.

Many TV shows from the 1980s are dated. I loved watching *Designing Women* during the Reagan-Bush years, but today, the four women from Atlanta don't hold up as well. My golden girls are timeless in their designer gowns. When the first season came out on DVD, I rushed right out and bought it.

Your heart is true. You're a pal and a confidante.

When I watched the show, I felt like I was watching my Nanny, Grandma, Mom, and me. I could fantasize endlessly about the four of us sharing a house, taking care of one another for as long as we could. These three women meant so much to me, it wouldn't have taken more than that for me to find the happiness I was seeking.

Just like my father, I sat on the couch pretending I was living in another time and place, one that didn't really exist anymore. Since I couldn't deal with my life, my DVDs and some junk food from the 7-Eleven were the closest things to my perfect companions.

I went back and forth between appealing to my mom and lashing out at Ted Haggard.

I still hadn't fully accepted the fact that my mother was gone. I needed to talk to her. I needed her advice, especially about what to do next with Ted Haggard.

I consider myself a Christian. I don't pray to a particular deity, and I don't envision my God as a man with long brown hair, a beard, and white robe when I pray. Perhaps I shouldn't call it prayer, because it's more like meditation or throwing a request out into the universe to see what answers come my way.

When in pain, lying in the fetal position can sometimes be the best way to ease it. Since discovering who Art really was, I'd been in pain. My stomach was tied up in knots, and I was all nerves. It seemed that I woke up every day with a migraine. I had started vomiting occasionally and that concerned me.

I would kneel in front of the couch with my arms folded on the cushions. I would clasp my hands together, but only so I could massage my fingers and my hands. There I was, on my knees, but not so I could worship God. I was sick. I began to feel dirty. I started questioning everything.

"What do I do? What do I do?" I pleaded. As I knelt on my living room floor, I thought of those paintings of Jesus in the Garden of Gethsemane, where he kneels in front of a rock and places his hands on it. I kept hoping beyond hope that a ray of light would beam down on me and tell me what to do, just like in those paintings. "I'm so lost," I cried.

When I stopped crying long enough, all I could hear was silence. That hurt. In frustration, I pounded my fists into the cushions. My tears literally drenched the couch, so not only did I still not know what to do, but my couch was now ruined.

Over the course of the next few days, my dreams started turning to Ted Haggard. His smiling face, his business-casual attire, his charming personality. I could almost see horns growing from his temples. It wasn't as if this was the first time I'd discovered something unpleasant about one of my clients. I had been with politicians, professional football players, and some of the biggest names in the world—all men who turned out to be less sure of themselves than their public personas might suggest. The main reason I never said anything—and still refuse to say anything about these other men—is that they have not, to my knowledge, done anything intentionally to hurt anyone else.

It was a different story with Ted. Here was the leader of 30 million evangelicals. Thirty million. That number astounded me. That's almost one-tenth of the entire population of the United States, and this man was their leader. Ten percent of a corporation can be enough to make you the largest shareholder. Ten percent of the population meant that you might really determine the future course of America. And that's what Ted Haggard was doing, all while enjoying gay porn and experimenting with sex toys on the side.

Ted was not like my other clients. Many, if not most, were hypocrites to some degree. We can all be hypocritical, if you think about it. The difference for me was that Ted was a very powerful hypocrite, one who could shape the nation's agenda by mere pronouncement. Bouncing around the World Wide Web, it became clear to me that gays, lesbians, and anyone else who was different would not fare well in one nation under Ted Haggard's god.

I had to do something, or at the very least, I had to say something. But the more I thought about it, the more I felt like I was David and Ted was Goliath. For starters, I was sure Ted had better lawyers and handlers. Hell, I didn't have even one lawyer or handler. I wasn't sure what course of action to take, and that's what was making me sick.

I kept thinking about his wife and children, because to me, they were the true victims of this situation. They would be caught right in the middle of it. Would I be blamed for their pain and suffering?

I wanted to talk to Ted, and yet I didn't want to talk to Ted. Every time the phone rang, I prayed to the universe that it would not be from a 719 area code. Often, it was just another client who wanted an hour of my time.

Before a client came over, I had to spend some time bringing myself out of my funk. I had every intention of returning to my funk once I was done, but prior to my appointment, I cleaned up and tried to pretend that everything was fine. I threw away the snack wrappers, fluffed the pillows, and tidied up. These men came to me to get away from their problems, not to deal with mine. Besides, it was a good distraction for me, if only a temporary one. Once my client left, I would plop back down on the couch and start crying again. When I did get up, it was either to throw up or to get on my knees and pray.

"Please, just tell me what to do," I asked my mother again.

"We think differently than the previous generation, the 1980s Moral Majority crowd," Ted said in the *Philadelphia Inquirer*.

Does this mean, Ted, that you are different from Jerry Falwell and Pat Robertson?

I spent the rest of the night and well into the morning bouncing around the Internet. I'd bookmark Web sites that had some good information that I either could not read or could not stomach at the time. I tried to get through them all, but it was exhausting. There was so much out there. "He's huge!" I said to myself, and I wasn't referring to his anatomy.

So big, in fact, that Tom Brokaw interviewed him in 2005 for a story called "In God They Trust" that aired on NBC. As Brokaw pointed out, "Ted Haggard believes that America is entering a new period of religious intensity that will alter both souls and society." Here's an excerpt from the interview:

> TOM BROKAW: What's the biggest misconception in the media, in the country, about the phenomenal rise, really, of the evangelical movement in America?
>
> TED HAGGARD: It's not political. It is authentically a spiritual renewal. And people are responding to the goodness of the scripture and the goodness of God's love, the assurance of eternal life. And so it's a spiritual renewal that's taking place and leading to the growth of churches that has political ramifications.
>
> BROKAW: What are the political ramifications?
>
> HAGGARD: Well, once people make a decision that God created them, then all of a sudden they value life. And they have a higher moral standard.

Occasionally, I had the strength to get up and go to the gym, but I was underperforming when I went. Instead of doing a ninety- or 120-minute workout, I'd barely do thirty minutes. Instead of lifting two hundred pounds, I was lucky to get seventy pounds off the ground. Sometimes, I'd get on the treadmill and just walk, feeling like I was recovering from hip replacement surgery. Other times, I'd just turn around and leave as soon as I got there. And when I got home, I either went to the couch or back to bed.

To be honest, I didn't cry anymore because my mother was gone. Now I cried because of *how* she died and for all the pain and suffering she had to endure on her way out of this universe. She hadn't gone peacefully. I've always been sensitive to other people's pain, which is why I did well in the escorting business. More often than not, my clients' pain became my pain. In a similar vein, all the pain that Ted was causing was becoming my pain. What a unique form of queer bashing.

My mom and dad's wedding anniversary came and went on April 17. It would have been their fifty-third. Some couples stay together because they're afraid to be apart, but my parents stayed together because they truly loved each other. I called my dad to say I was thinking of him, and then I picked up a photo I'd taken of my parents some years earlier and realized that, in my eyes, my dad was still a strapping young sergeant and my mom a beautiful young entertainer.

It was May 7. Happy birthday, Mike, I said to myself. I was awake, fresh from the gym and a huge breakfast, and I was sitting on the couch. I wasn't crying or eating pastries, so that was an improvement. But then I realized that I was waiting for my mom to call, which she always did for as long as she was alive, even when she was in so much pain the year before, to wish me a happy birthday and tell me she loved me. Once again, I started crying uncontrollably.

I admit that my crying did make me feel better. They say that tears wash toxins from your body, so all this crying was a great start. I suddenly remembered one family vacation in the Rockies when my mother had fallen asleep while Dad was driving along one of those unpaved mountain roads. When he stopped at a cattle crossing and rolled down all the windows, a cow poked her head through the passenger window and started licking Mom's face, waking her up in a panic. We all laughed until we cried.

By the time Mother's Day arrived, the day I had been dreading more than any other, it was a bit easier for me to leave behind my grieving and remember how we'd celebrated in past years. I always sent her roses. Whether I bought her perfume or earrings, I could never go wrong. Her favorite fragrances were White Diamonds and Red Door. If I bought her a set of earrings, she would put them on right away. And she was never happier than when she got flowers, perfume, *and* earrings.

Finally, as I sat on the couch, some justice came into the world.

Kenneth Lay and Jeffrey Skilling of Enron Corporation fame were found guilty in May. When you're depressed like I was, something like that can really put you in a good mood. I took it as an opportunity to feel better about the world. That time, I believe my happiness lasted for almost an hour.

A friend called and invited me to a Tony Awards party that was coming up in June, but I said no. I had a client that night, I told him. That may have been true—I don't remember. I just remember lying on the couch watching another batch of *Modern Marvels* installments on the History Channel. I knew I was not feeling well when I preferred that to watching something live on Broadway.

Ted Haggard's face was still front and center in my brain. I was putting myself through hell over what to do. *Do I go to his church and confront him? Do I take pictures of him having sex? Do I call his wife?* Then I started pondering the one option that I hadn't thought about much. *Perhaps I should just say nothing.* I mean, was all this crap worth it? All it was doing was making me depressed and interfering with my normal life. I felt I owed it to the community, but really, would any good come of making this public? If so, why was it *my* responsibility?

A massage client was coming in a few hours. Time to sparkle. That day I needed at least a couple of hours to get my poker face ready. With my luck, I would come forward about me and Ted Haggard, get my fifteen minutes of fame, and then wind up on daytime television with Jeff Skilling and Kenneth Lay.

Back on the Internet, I discovered that Ted had traveled to Israel with a group of Evangelical leaders to see about leasing some space for another megachurch. He made that trip around the same time that he'd first asked me how he could get some meth. Apparently, Ted Haggard was even a big shot internationally.

The first time I saw Ted after I'd learned who he was required extra preparation. I patted down my hair and pretended to press the wrinkles out of my clothes. I dabbed my eyes with a tissue just to make sure they had no tears. I kept rubbing my mouth, hoping I wouldn't say something or do something that would blow my cover.

"Hi, Mike," Ted said as he opened his arms for me.

I smiled and let him kiss me on the cheek and squeeze me very tight.

"It's so great to see you again," Ted said enthusiastically. I wondered if he told his wife that, too.

"It's good to see you, too, T . . . Art," I replied mechanically. Why the hell did I say that?

Ted did a quick snort of meth before we got started. I turned off the few remaining lights in my apartment, and then, as usual and as requested, I lit one small tea candle in the massage room. I undressed completely and stood by the foot of the massage table waiting for him. He came in, took off his clothes, and lay face down on the massage table. Just as almost every other time, I stood naked in front of his face and reached out my hands to massage his back while he rubbed his face in my dick.

After about ten minutes of that, he hopped off the massage table, buck naked, and opened his backpack. Out came a new collection of sex toys that he wanted to play with.

Ted began fumbling around with what I think was a vibrator. I kept hearing a small motor go on and off.

"Mike, could you help me?" he asked. It was a good thing the room was so dark because that meant I didn't have to hide the expression on my face. *Yes, Ted, I'd love to shove something up your ass! How 'bout some honesty?* I took the vibrator and greased it up while he put some lube inside his rectum. I carefully inserted it until I could sense his enjoyment.

"Hey, handsome, does this feel good to you?"

He moaned with pleasure. Well, at least he was enjoying himself. Then, as usual, I jacked him off. I found it ironic: I literally had him by the balls, and yet I could do nothing to him. Moments later, he ejaculated. I gave him a hand towel, and he wiped himself off. Then he scurried to the bathroom and closed the door behind him.

There, in the darkness of the massage room, I started to cry. This man was torturing me, and he didn't even know it. How I wished that a camera crew would magically appear while he was in the bathroom. I picked up the towel he had used and threw it in the laundry basket. Then I grabbed a tissue and wiped my eyes. If he noticed that I was crying, I would tell him that I was still upset about my mother's death.

"I really enjoy being with you," he said to me, money in hand and lips extended for a kiss.

I was finding it hard to muster a smile. I kissed him, rubbed his shoulder, and took the money.

"You always make me feel so good!"

Oh, save it, buddy!

"Looking forward to next time, Mike." With a big grin and eyes open wide, he sauntered down the hallway to the elevator.

I closed the door immediately after he was over the threshold. Less than a minute later, I heard the elevator door open. One moment more, and I knew he was gone.

"You goddamn hypocrite!" I yelled, raising my fist and punching the plasterboard wall in my living room. That wasn't the smartest thing for me to do, because my hand and arm hurt a bit from the impact. I shuffled over to my leather rocker and plopped myself into it. As expected, I started crying—again.

Do I tell him that I know who he is? Do I call the media?

I was dealing with a force much bigger than me. How the hell could I possibly win against someone like Pastor Ted?

Whenever I needed a laugh, I pulled up a picture of Ted Haggard wearing a Hawaiian lei and holding his hands up to the heavens in prayer. He looked ridiculous. It was one of the only things about him that brought a smile to my face. The article that went along with the photo read: "Ted Haggard's name is not yet a household word like Billy Graham, but he's getting there," according to the *Honolulu Star-Bulletin*.

Yeah, well, you may be powerful, but you look silly! Oh boy, that made me feel better!

I had survived a metal door falling on me. I had survived baseball bats to the head. I had survived constant beatings from my brother. I would survive my mother's painful death. And I would survive Ted Haggard. I had to keep telling myself that, because with each passing day I believed less and less that I really would survive.

I was fortunate never to have contracted HIV. Still, I'd lost a lot of friends to AIDS. During the 1980s and early 1990s, when people were dying every day, there was a huge stigma associated with AIDS and HIV. People were afraid to touch someone with AIDS. Fear spread like fire, and it angered me that as my friends and acquaintances were dying, few people wanted to hold them or touch them, including their relatives.

Possibly the best thing I provided for my friends during their final days was—you guessed it—massage. It was during this time in my life that I learned how correct my Nanny, my great-grandmother, was about the healing power of massage. These men were nothing but skin and bones, and they were hurting for the touch of another person.

I would take my massage table over to their houses and rub their ailing bodies for hours. I could do any type of massage, but what they really needed was just a gentle touch. You could almost see them come back to life once I touched them. Even some of their friends couldn't stand to touch them, but it was no problem for me. This wasn't sex, it was healing. So many people just don't understand that.

When I remember the politics of the Reagan-Bush years, which kept AIDS a dirty little secret, I still get angry to this day. When I think of how much pain my mother endured, I get even angrier that we don't have more effective treatments for cancer. And then I think of how powerful leaders, both religious and political, use their words to cut down people like me. My blood pressure goes through the roof.

I was feeling helpless, and I hated that feeling. I could give my friends a massage, but I couldn't prevent their deaths. I could make my mother laugh, but I couldn't keep her alive. And I could give pleasure to someone like Ted Haggard, but I couldn't stop him from gay bashing.

The final vote on the Marriage Amendment was 49 to 48, and Dick Cheney could do nothing about it. The proposed amendment had been defeated.

Once again, attempts to write marriage into the United States Constitution had failed. But not to fear, they'll be back. The threat of two women or two men getting legally married is too great to ignore for long. Next thing you know, they'll be wanting equal rights.

I was of course happy that the amendment went down, but I was still bothered. After awhile, most people give up, but not these religious zealots. The Ted Haggards of the world aren't happy until they've browbeaten everyone into their way of thinking. "Do as I say, not as I do." If everyone did as Ted Haggard did, I would be tired, but I would be one very rich man.

Some nights I would wake up and find myself almost mummified in my own sheets. Other nights I would be breathing so hard and sweating so profusely that my pillows would be drenched, and the air would almost choke me.

And then those goddamn migraines would start. How I hated those headaches. It was bad enough that I was hurting and vomiting and crying, but on top of all of that, my head felt like a stack of bricks. Would there be no escape from Ted Haggard hell?

"Hey, handsome!"

God, I couldn't muster even a half-smile. I gave him a hug and left him alone to do his hit of meth. I shuffled off to the massage room and undressed lifelessly. Standing in the low light waiting for him, I no longer had the energy to mentally berate him for being a hypocrite. I was too exhausted.

"Can we watch a little porn?" he asked as he stood fully clothed in the doorway.

Can't you see I have a headache? I put my clothes back on and joined him on the couch for another round of hot man-on-man action. Fortunately, our porn viewing lasted only a few minutes before he was ready to get naked. *Oh please, God, make this night an easy one!*

Pulling several small leather toys and a penis pump out of his bag of tricks, he spent the rest of the hour playing with himself as I watched. I was so grateful I didn't have to do anything that session. My most exciting thought that day was that maybe I'd go to the grocery store with the two hundred dollars and buy some real food.

After he left, I went to the bathroom to throw up. It all came up, everything I had ingested over the last few days, including the sleeping pills I had started taking. Light-headed, I went to the couch and lied down. I wanted to be free of my pain, and continuing to see Ted wasn't helping. I had to do something, but I had no idea what.

I was fortunate enough to have a few close friends who were there for me before and after my mother died. I had offers of dinner or a movie and was invited to come over just to sit and have a little tea and sympathy. But as spring turned to summer and summer heated up, the wear and tear on me was hard to miss. My friends aren't stupid. They knew something was really eating at me, but they probably figured it was all about my mother. I wanted so much to share my entire story with them, but I couldn't. Ever since I was a kid, I felt I had no one to rely on but myself. As I wrestled with my demons,

I knew I had plenty of people who would help me, but, well, I just didn't want to bother them.

Despite my best efforts, my face was telling a much bigger story than I realized. Rather than spill the beans, I stopped seeing my friends altogether. I knew they felt slighted, but I felt I had no choice. I didn't know what was going to happen, if anything. Regardless, I didn't want them to be a party to whatever hornet's nest I might stir up. My friends deserved better than to get dragged down by my troubles, which were looking bleaker by the minute.

"You're okay staying home tonight?"

"I'm fine," my father said. Dad had come to Denver for my niece's wedding and was staying with me for ten days. He was so entranced by the episode of *Diagnosis Murder* he was watching that he barely looked up when I spoke to him.

"I promise I won't make any noise," I told him, getting the massage room ready. Once my client buzzed the apartment, I moved my father from the living room to my bedroom, where I had *Diagnosis Murder* all ready to go on the television on my dresser. He sat in there with the door closed, a glass of water, and Dick Van Dyke. My client waited patiently at the door while I got ready. I greeted him and told him that my father was in the next room, so please be quiet.

When the hour was up, I took a shower and then walked in on Dad, who was now watching *Ironside*. "Are you ready for dinner?" I asked him, wiping my hair with a towel.

"I'm not hungry tonight," he said. Nothing seemed to be wrong, so I didn't press him.

I loved having my father around, even though we said very little to each other. That's just how our relationship was. Earlier in the week, I'd taken him to a dinner theater, and he seemed to enjoy that. I also took him to a Colorado Rockies game, and he really enjoyed that, even though the home team lost big time.

I knew he was depressed, but he would never admit it. I handled him just like I handled my clients. If you don't tell me, I won't ask.

"Mike, I'm downtown. Can I come see you?"

Of all the times for him to call, I thought.

"Is everything okay, Mike?" my father asked.

"Everything's fine, Dad," I told him. "Finish watching your show."

I went into my bedroom and closed the door. "Art, I just can't, not tonight."

"Could I just swing by and give you a hug?" Ted insisted. "I'd really love to see you before I go back home."

My mind was racing. I wanted to beat him up and berate him and take his money. But all I said was, "I can give you five minutes but no more. My father is in town for a visit."

"Oh, bless you," Ted said. *Bless me? Phooey!*

After I hung up, my upper lip started quivering, and I started feeling like shit again.

"Dad, I have to go take care of something real quick," I said as I grabbed my keys. "It won't take long."

My father said nothing as he enjoyed another rerun of one of his favorite television shows.

I stood outside my building with my arms crossed waiting for Ted to show up. It would have been a perfect time for some photos of Ted enjoying all the nightlife that gay Capitol Hill had to offer.

"Hi," Ted said as he popped out of nowhere with a big smile.

I kept my arms crossed, but I played it off as though it were chilly. I took him inside and looked around. I could take him downstairs to the pool and sauna area, but that might be too obvious. I looked in the small billiards room off to the left and saw no one, so I decided that that was where we were going to do whatever it was he wanted to do.

I had him follow me into the small room with a pool table and closed the door behind us. Without saying a word, he gently pushed me up against the wall. Immediately, he pulled down my gym shorts and got on his knees. I think you can guess what he did from there.

I let him go on for about ten minutes. I wasn't turned on at all—how could I be?—but Ted didn't seem to mind. He just wanted to touch me.

"We better stop," I said. Not that I would have been the first man to be caught in a homosexual act in a public space in my building.

Ted stood up and wiped his mouth with a tissue. "Mike, I just want to touch you so badly," he said with heavy breath. "You know how much I like that."

Without missing a beat, he kissed me on the cheek, reached into his pocket, and handed me two hundred dollars. "You'd better go," I said as though I were concerned someone might see him. It was only then that I realized that he'd just given me a blow job with the lights on. He was either maturing or getting sloppy.

"I really needed that," he said as he rubbed me all over. "Thank you, thank you, thank you." He was taking forever to say good-bye.

Seeing him leave the building both relieved and worried me. How long could this go on? What if I reached a breaking point and snapped at the wrong moment? I summoned the elevator and went back to my apartment. "Let's go eat, Dad," I said.

We went to the Village Inn, which is where we'd gone the past three nights. Dad liked eating there; the food was tasty and the ambiance enjoyable. We didn't say much to each other. He had little to say, and I had nothing that I wanted him to know. We sat and enjoyed each other's company.

"What are you going to do when you get back to California?" I asked him.

"I don't know, Mike," he responded. "One day at a time, I guess."

The next day I took Dad to Denver International Airport and put him on a plane back to California. I tried to make his departure as routine and low key as possible, but as we got closer to the departure gates area, we both starting getting emotional.

"You're a wonderful son, Michael," my father told me, giving me the biggest hug he could muster. "Thank you for all you've done for your mother and me."

I was about to burst into tears, so I said a quick good-bye and waved to him as he got into the security-check line. Then I turned back toward my car, which was parked in the garage. At first I was walking, but then I began running. I got in my Pontiac and just started bawling. I sat there for about ten minutes, unable to drive.

Checking my phone messages when I got home, there was one from a 719 area code. I froze, but the caller turned out to be someone else from Colorado Springs. The last time I'd seen him, he'd confided in me that he worked for one of the ultra-conservative churches down there.

"I know it's late at night, but can you still see me?" he said on his message. "I'll pay extra." He sounded desperate, just like Ted Haggard. Last time, he'd paid me in ones and fives. I couldn't help but think it was money from the collection plate. Where *do* these guys get the money to come see me? Extreme Christianity pays better than you would think.

It was coming up on Independence Day, so I decided to throw a party.

When I was a kid in Edgewater, there were all kinds of fireworks shows to celebrate the Fourth of July. The weather was always warm. Mom would prepare chicken, or Dad would barbeque hamburgers. We would sit in our backyard and watch the sky light up in all directions. It was one of my all-American, middle-class memories.

By the time July 4 rolled around in 2006, I had already celebrated my forty-ninth birthday and survived a series of important dates without my mother: Mother's Day, her birthday, and her wedding anniversary. Nothing was going right. Even though it was summertime, it seemed like the days just kept getting shorter and darker. I hoped throwing a party would cheer me up.

My apartment has a great view, and on July 4 there are all kinds of fireworks throughout the city. There must have been about twenty people in my apartment, all celebrating summer and the long weekend. I provided chicken and potato salad and many summer picnic items, followed by pie and cake. I wanted to have fun, and I wanted the people I loved to have fun, too. Perhaps if I could make them happy, it would spark some happiness within me. My mother got the most out of life by making sure others were having a good time. That night, I hoped her life strategy would also work for me.

Yet after a couple of hours of a painted smile and no discussion about what was really going on in my life, I realized that all my efforts to be happy were in vain. Part of it was my mother, but a bigger part of it was the puzzle of Ted Haggard. I just could not get his smiling face out of my mind. One moment he's smiling with joy over seeing me and the next minute he's got his finger pointed at me and my friends, telling us how immoral we are. In spite of my anger at him, I found it interesting that he could float from one end of the morality scale to the other. My emotions can be like a roller coaster, too, but I always felt that my actions were consistent with my beliefs. With someone like Ted, there was no consistency— and yet he pulled it off so well.

I slipped into my bedroom and started bawling again. How many tears could one person cry? I had done nothing but cry and be sick for almost three months, and I wondered how long I could go on before things collapsed. I could see myself getting sick and going to the emergency room, or worse yet, I imagined that I'd be in public somewhere and I'd go off on someone just because they looked at me the wrong way. I was becoming more volatile.

"Damn you, Ted Haggard!" I said repeatedly, pounding my fist into the bed. I wasn't even trying to be quiet about it, and my carelessness was a sign that I was getting ready to crack. "Because of people like you, my friends out there can't enjoy the rights you take for granted!" I could only imagine what Ted would say about my friends at the party having too much to drink, and that pissed me off even more, knowing that he did meth and thought nothing of it. Maybe he thought it was different because he was doing it out of public view, in front of a nobody like me.

I felt that Ted was laughing at me. I wanted to fight back. "Ted, you should be ashamed of yourself!" I scolded him, but a lot of good that did me.

I'd been in my room almost twenty minutes before I real-

ized that I had to get back to my party. I wanted to tell someone of my pain, but that night, July 4, was not the time or the
place. All I could think of was Mr. Roarke on *Fantasy Island*
saying, "Smiles, everyone, smiles." I wiped my eyes as dry as
I could get them, clutched the bedroom doorknob, turned it,
and pulled. Charades, anyone?

"It's really pretty hard not to like Ted Haggard," John
Stevens, a retired pastor of the First Presbyterian Church in
Colorado Springs, told a local paper. "You can not like some
of the things he does, or some of the things he might say on
occasion, but it's pretty hard not to like him personally."

"Aren't these fun?" Ted said as he pulled the cock ring around
his scrotum.

He was like a kid in a candy store with all these sex toys.
He was having fun, but I was so out of it, my eyes had glazed
over. I put my finger inside the cock ring to try to adjust it so
his balls wouldn't get pinched.

"I'm so glad you turned me on to all these toys," he
exclaimed, using the same voice of excitement he had used on
the Joni Lamb show just months earlier. "I've missed you,
Mike."

I steered my mind to happier thoughts, anything that
would get me through our session. Rather than think about
what I would like to do to Ted, I imagined him as a hunky
schoolteacher who wanted his young student to show him
what he had learned in fitness class. That fantasy worked
enough to get me to smile, but just a little.

Ted was enjoying it all. I got him off as quickly as I could
and almost pushed him into the bathroom so he could change
and leave.

God, I couldn't believe I was actually fantasizing about beating up Ted, right there in front of him. The thought scared me. I wanted to beat him up, and at the same time, I didn't want anything bad to happen to him. I just wanted him to know how much pain he was causing me and so many other people, including his family.

I wiped my eyes and waited for him in the living room. He came out of the bathroom fully dressed, handed me my money, kissed me, and left. There was even a big tip for all my efforts and sorrows.

I went back into the massage room to clean up. I started stripping the sheets from the massage table. Angry over everything, I yanked the sheets off and wadded them up furiously. I strangled the ball of sheets and started punching it.

As my hand went right through the sheets and into the massage table, I knew I had been defeated. I just couldn't fight anymore. I collapsed in tears on the floor. Ted had won. He had risen. I had lost and was descending into hell, though it felt like I was already in hell.

I went to my computer, and the Web site for a local television station was staring back at me. I had visited the site earlier to see what was happening locally. Off to the side was a link to a profile of their star investigative reporter. I clicked on it and read it. I read it over and over again.

If I alerted the media, would anyone believe me? I imagined the questions I would face: "How did you meet him, Mr. Jones? Reverend Haggard paid you for sex, you say? So that means that you're nothing more than a whore?"

My friend Lloyd Peltzer's birthday had come and gone, and I hadn't taken him to dinner or done anything special for him. Lloyd lives in the Rocky Mountains and comes to Denver about once a week. So the next time he called to say when he would be in Denver, I invited him to dinner for his birthday.

Lloyd knew I had been uptight for the last few months, but I told him it was depression related to my mother's death. He told me he wasn't buying it and wanted me to tell him everything. I told him I couldn't, that at some point I would tell him why. He reassured me that I had his complete support, regardless.

At dinner, without naming names, I told him that I had been "seeing someone" (Lloyd didn't know that I was an escort) and that this man was a powerful church leader. I told him that I was not sure what to do with this information.

"Mike, you know what's best," Lloyd told me. "Do what you feel is right." Then he asked, "Have you seen a therapist?"

I took another bite of my steak and wondered what to make of his comments.

"Well, have you seen one?" he asked again.

I told him my problems were all inside my head and that I was addressing them as best I could.

CHAPTER 9

GOING TO THE MEDIA

❖

On August 4, 2006, at 2:17 p.m., Ted left me the following voice mail:

> Hi Mike, this is Art. Hey, I was just calling to see if we could get any more, either [a] one-hundred- or two-hundred-dollar supply, and I could pick it up really at any time. I could get it tomorrow, or we could wait until next week some time. And so, I also wanted to get your address so I could send you some money for inventory, but obviously that's not working. And so if you have it, then go ahead and get what you can, and I may buzz up there, I don't know, maybe even later today. But I doubt your schedule would allow that, unless you have some in the house. Okay, so I'll check back in with you later. Thanks a lot. Bye.

He had never left such a detailed message before. He was always so careful to disguise anything that might give away his true identity. I listened to his message a couple of times. The desperation in his voice was obvious. He needed some meth, and he needed it right away.

There was no way I was going to get involved. I'd pushed my luck just putting him in touch with Todd in the first place. I hadn't heard from Todd in more than a year, and I wasn't going to track him down, especially now that I knew Art was really Ted. I was so angry. I was still not sure what I would do, if anything. I really didn't want to see or hear from Ted again.

Rather than erase my voice mail messages like I normally did, something told me not to press seven to erase it. Instead, I pushed nine to save it.

Then my phone rang. It was Ted again. He wanted to know if I could "score" him some "more." I told him I would see what I could do.

Something about his call left me feeling uncomfortable. I had to turn my thinking around quickly, so I grabbed a pair of dumbbells and started pumping out bicep curls. It's a quick way to burn off some energy and distract yourself. After a couple of sets, I got on the floor and did about forty push-ups. The jolt to my bloodstream made me feel better.

I stepped out to get some groceries, and while I was out Ted called again. He left this voice mail message at 5:10 p.m. on the same day, August 4:

> Hi Mike, this is Art. Hey, I am here in Denver and sorry that I missed you, but as I said, if you want to go ahead and get some stuff, then that would be great, and then I will get it sometime next week or the week after or whatever. I will call you, though, early next week to see what's most convenient for you. Okay, thanks a lot. Bye.

The universe was telling me something. This guy couldn't leave me alone, and he was so desperate that he was leaving me some pretty incriminating voice mails. Once again, I decided to save the message.

A day later, he called again, asking for my mailing address. He'd been to my apartment more than a dozen times, but apparently he could not remember my exact street address or apartment number. I gave him my address, but my gut was telling me there was something to fear.

I was trying to get back to leading a normal daily life. I was proud that I was making it to the gym every day and that I'd stopped making thrice-daily runs to 7-Eleven. But my mood still hadn't improved. I still felt I had to do something about Ted, but I didn't know what. I still feared him, though I couldn't say why. I kept wishing it would all go away and that Ted would go with it.

A few days later, I received a letter in the mail postmarked Colorado Springs, August 7, 2006. In the upper left-hand corner was the word "Art" written in blue ink and big capital letters.

I took my mail upstairs and sat at my dining room table. The first thing I opened carefully was that envelope. Inside, wrapped in a plain white piece of paper, were two hundred-dollar bills. There was no writing on the paper. I knew the letter came from Ted. I knew that the money was for me to get him some meth. What else could it be? He had never prepaid for sex. On the front of the envelope, "Mike" was written in blue ink, while my last name and address were written in black ink. The letter had a meter stamp on it instead of a regular stamp.

Fuck you, Ted.

There was no way I was going to follow through with his request.

Without saying a word, Ted entered my apartment and immediately pressed himself against me, stroking me as if I were one big penis that he wanted to stimulate.

I was too shell-shocked to say anything. I had gotten little sleep, and when I did sleep I dreamed about him or my mother. I was not in the mood for anything. I certainly was not in the mood to entertain him.

"Let's watch some porn," I told him, grabbing his hand and taking him over to the couch.

"What about the meth?" he asked.

It was a good thing that he was so focused on himself that he could not see the anger in my face. "I'll see what I can do." I cracked an incredibly fake smile. "Let's sit down and, you know, make . . ." I couldn't even think straight.

That was okay, though. Ted was in another world, and if he truly had feelings for me, this was one time I could play it to my advantage.

We sat on the couch and watched some pretty hardcore gay porn, the kind that shows sex acts that can be performed only by the extremely limber. Ted kept rubbing my chest. "I'd love to have a chest like yours," he said. "Show me some more weight-lifting exercises."

Oh, hell. I grudgingly took him over to the workout bench, sat him down, and put a set of dumbbells in his hands that were obviously too heavy for him. After he struggled trying to do just one curl, I grabbed the weights from him and knocked them down a few pounds. He did several bicep curls, but his form was poor. I showed him the correct way to do it, and he did a few more reps.

"Let's go to the massage room," I recommended. I took him firmly by the hand and took off his clothes for him. I knew that was not how he liked to do things, but I didn't care. I was getting angrier by the minute.

Once naked, I rushed him onto the massage table and, without asking, began to jack him off. He wasn't fighting me. In fact, he seemed to be enjoying it.

But after five minutes, he wasn't even hard. I took my mind

to happier places, envisioning Ted in a Hawaiian lei. That slowed me down enough to just stand there and rub him all over.

"Is something wrong?" he asked.

"My mother," I quickly said.

He said nothing and let it go at that. A few minutes later, he was up, dressed, and out the door. Maybe he would get the hint and not come back anymore.

Yet a few days later, Ted was back, and I knew he was coming for meth—not sex.

I greeted him at the door with a bottle of water.

"Did you get it?" he asked with excitement.

"No, I did not, Art." I needed to be as calm and forceful as possible. "It's not going to happen right now. I'm sorry."

The disappointment on his face was scary. His expression was similar to that of desperate junkies when they can't get a fix. He put down the water bottle and shuffled off to the massage room for what would be our last session.

We were both in a bad mood, and it was pretty obvious. Neither of us were stimulated. He couldn't get hard and his hands were more limp than titillating. My hand movements were just as lame. After only twenty minutes, he got up and put his clothes on. He gave me a quick hug and said, "Keep trying, okay?"

I said nothing and closed the door behind him. I went to the couch and closed my eyes. I was feeling more torn than ever.

"Sodomy is a violation of God's law," wrote Ted in *Ministry Today Magazine* in 2004, "and Christians are justifiably upset about the legalization of the practice." He continued:

But we are faced with an age-old dilemma: At what point is it appropriate to enforce our moral convictions upon the unwilling through the power of the state?

Should people who commit adultery be put in prison because of their immoral influence?

Finally, I'd had enough. I pulled up the Web site for KUSA-TV. I had to say something. I had to do something.

About twenty years ago, I'd had a brief encounter with Paula Woodward, an investigative news reporter at Channel 9, the local NBC affiliate. I'd met her outside a business where she was talking with a friend of mine. He introduced me to her, and she seemed nice, not at all standoffish. That chance meeting stayed in my mind. I remember thinking that if I ever needed to talk to a reporter, she would be a good one to talk to.

Paula had been a reporter in Denver for almost thirty years. Ask anyone to name a reporter on a Denver television station, and her name will most likely come up. She is a Denver institution. Perhaps she could help me. I sent her this e-mail on August 15:

I am a 49 year-old gay man. I have lived in Denver all my life. I was a gay escort for many years. I have been with pro athletes, politicians, movie stars, and lots of clergy. I have always kept my encounters confidential. I am not the type to out people. But right now I am really struggling. I have seen this one man for several years. He showed all the classic characteristics of clergy but he never talked about it and I could not verify. Then a few months ago I was watching the History channel on religion. And to my surprise there he was as an expert. I could not catch his name and church [and] before I could get myself together his name was gone. Then the next morning I am at the gym and for some strange reason the religious channel was on. This was not normal. But as I am on the treadmill, there he is again talking with a lady named "Joni." The bottom line is I have found out he heads one of the largest Christian organizations in the country and is preaching antigay marriage information. But he is having gay relations behind his flock. This is so wrong. What a hypocrite.

To my surprise, she wrote back within a few hours: "I am very interested and you will remain anonymous. Thank you for writing to me. What would you like to do now? I'm glad you wrote."

She included her pager and cell phone number. I called her right back to schedule a meeting. We were all set to meet two weeks later.

I was delighted that she wanted to talk with me, but as you can imagine, I had to think about what I was going to do. Now that I'd called her, even without naming names, suddenly my secret was out. If I mentioned Ted's name, it would be the first time I ever violated a client's trust. And if I told her about Ted, I would have to tell her about me. I couldn't imagine her seeing me as a dirty whore, but I could imagine her feeling uncomfortable. The last thing I wanted to do was make anyone feel uncomfortable around me.

I reread Ted's sermons on sodomy and adultery. I was still very angry, but now that I was going forward, I began to question if I was doing the right thing. This could destroy him, I feared, and that wasn't what I wanted.

On the morning of my meeting with Paula, I took the voice mail tapes and the envelope to the Channel 9 studio. I didn't take the money Ted sent because I had already spent it. Paula met me at the reception desk and, before we started talking, took me on a quick tour of the studio. Then we walked to a conference room, and my heart started pounding faster.

After a few formalities, I poured my heart out to her. I played the voice mail tapes, showed her the envelope, gave her the entire history of Art as a client. I just didn't tell her who Art was.

She seemed unimpressed. Maybe that's just how reporters are, but I felt that we hadn't connected. If she was intrigued, she had one of the best poker faces I'd ever seen, even better than my mother's.

"Okay, okay," I finally said. "It's Ted Haggard." From my portfolio, I pulled out all the material I'd printed off the Internet. I specifically wanted her to take note of what I'd printed off Ted's Web page, where it said he was "president of the thirty million member National Association of Evangelicals."

"He became president a few months before he first saw me three years ago," I told her.

Paula took a few minutes to read the papers I'd given her. She turned each page slowly, seemingly unconcerned with time. "Wait right here," she told me.

I sat there dumbfounded. There was nothing but silence all around. Had I just spilled my guts for nothing?

A few minutes later, Paula walked back into the conference room with two other people: her boss, Patti Dennis, the news director, and Tim Ryan, the assistant news director.

"I need as many heads on this as possible," Paula said.

All three sat and listened intently as I told my story again.

One of the first questions they asked was why I was coming forward with this information. Fair enough, I felt.

"I am doing this to expose the hypocrisy of Ted Haggard," I stated firmly. "I want to do this before the election, so, yes, I am doing this for political reasons." I was up front about that.

Paula had me retell how I'd been seeing Ted, who I knew as Art, for the last three years and how we had sex about once a month, for which he paid me two hundred dollars each time.

"So you got paid for sex?" one of them asked.

I was caught off guard a bit. "Yes, I am a gay escort," I replied. I went on to tell them how Ted used meth before we had sex and how just days ago he asked me to get some for him. "I'd like this story to come out before the elections," I added. "In fact, a debate between Ted and me might be good."

No one said a word; they were seemingly unfazed by what I said.

Then I showed them the tapes I had of his voice mails and the envelope he sent.

All three leaned forward in their chairs to examine the evidence.

Finally, all three lightened up a bit. Before long, our conversation turned into a brainstorming session. I was right in there with them, discussing how we could get more evidence of Ted and me having sex. It was going better than I thought.

Then the mood turned serious again.

"Thank you for coming in, Mike," Paula said. I felt doomed. "You're talking about illegal activity here," she said, referring to the meth use by Ted and the fact that I was soliciting. "You need to get an attorney for your own protection."

That came out of nowhere for me. I said I would find one and wanted to move on. "What about my story?" I asked.

Unfortunately, there wasn't much to move on to, as far as the three of them were concerned. No doubt, they wanted my story, but they felt there was nothing with which to move forward. After discussing the situation some more, it was obvious that they would have preferred videotape to an audio recording.

They were just like a bunch of lawyers. They could not give me any particulars. They were very noncommittal, though they did tell me they thought it was a good story.

I told them that Ted should be calling me any day now. "Shall I call you when he calls me?" I asked.

Yes, that would be good, they said. All three started to gather up their things, signaling that the meeting was over.

I, too, gathered my things, feeling hurt and rejected. I wanted so much to have them put a camera in my face and let me tell the world what a hypocrite Ted Haggard was. Instead, I got a cold shower of reality.

Paula showed me out of the studio, thanking me for coming in.

"You do believe me, don't you?" I asked her.

Paula, always the professional, smiled. "It's not about whether or not I believe you," she replied. "Certain things have to be in place before we can air any story," she told me. "This story isn't there yet."

I thanked her and headed home. I wanted to give her a hug because that's what I usually do, regardless of the setting. Instead, I shook her hand. In my heart, I knew that getting some more evidence should not be that difficult, yet the pressure of actually getting it was weighing on me.

Paula had to make sure the story was "accurate," which meant that the story had to match the facts and that all the pieces, or at least enough pieces, whatever they were, had to be in place. She was less concerned with "truth," implying that some people's truths weren't necessarily factual. I was getting confused, but I think I understood her logic. She just needed to cover her ass.

That weekend, I kept going over in my head what they had told me. I was disappointed by their response and frustrated by their lack of direction as to how we could move this story forward. I really did not understand why the tapes and the envelope were not enough evidence.

"Just tell me what you want, and I'll get it for you!" I shouted to myself. After that outburst, I put my hands to my head and cried. Not only had I betrayed Art's trust, now I was getting ready to set him up.

Not sure what to do, I borrowed a video camera from a friend. I placed it in a chair in a corner and had it ready to go, complete with a charged battery and fresh videotape. I wasn't sure how I was going to use it, but at least I was ready.

After the three-day weekend, Paula called me and said they needed to get me on tape stating my allegations. I agreed, and within a couple of hours, she and a cameraman showed up at my apartment to get my story.

Paula asked me some very direct questions regarding sex with Ted Haggard and the drugs he used. I answered them directly and honestly. Again, I said that I had had a three-year relationship with Ted Haggard and that I had seen him approximately once a month during that time. I also explained that about a year into the relationship he asked me if I could get him some meth. I admitted to finding a connection for him to obtain the meth. I've never denied that.

After about twenty minutes, they packed up their stuff and headed out. Paula said she would be in touch. For a moment I was very excited. Finally, there was some progress. But just as quickly as they popped in and popped out, I started feeling alone again. They were waiting for something to happen. I was waiting for something to happen. Here it was September, and it felt like nothing was ever going to happen again.

"He should be calling me any day now," I assured Paula. She told me that a camera crew was ready to come to my apartment building. All I had to do was call her once I had scheduled an appointment with Art. "Hang in there," she told me.

Paula was patient as the days wore on with no sign of Ted. I started apologizing to her for Ted's inaction. In my heart, I felt that I was letting her down, even though it was all out of my control. I yearned for the couch again.

"He should be calling anytime, really," I told her. Every time my phone rang, I would quickly check my caller ID to see if it was a blocked call or if it was from a 719 phone number. Sometimes, when it was a 719 area code, my heart would start pounding wildly. But each time, it was not Ted.

Time wore on. We notched thirty days from my first meeting at Channel 9 and still no sign of the Reverend Haggard. "I swear, this is not like him," I told her. I wanted so badly to call Paula and ask her if she believed me. Other than her bosses, she was the only one I'd ever told about my life as an escort. My closest friends did not know what she knew. I needed to know that everything would be all right. Day in and day out, I was sure of less and less. All the while, I felt like I was setting a trap, and I felt trapped myself. My mental health was deteriorating.

I was still spending several hours daily digging up information about Ted Haggard on the Web. It was my new addiction, an attempt to replace junk food and *The Golden Girls*.

Ted knew a lot of famous people: Tom Brokaw, Barbara Walters, Mel Gibson, Chris Matthews, and all kinds of political figures, including George W. Bush. Ted had even met with British Prime Minister Tony Blair to talk about the environment. It'd be easy to think Ted was a decent guy—as long as you never read his sermons.

Part of my searches always included taking a look at www.tedhaggard.com and the New Life Church Web site. Bouncing around the church's site one night, I discovered that on October 20 and 21, New Life would be having a men's retreat in the south Denver metro area. I started bouncing with joy, because I knew that was something Ted would be attending. I called Paula right away, even though it was almost ten o'clock. I gave her the details and told her, "I can't imagine Ted not sneaking away for a moment to come see me."

Paula told me she would let her bosses know and thanked me for calling. I hung up, almost giddy with excitement. Something like that can suddenly make you feel like a winner, just like the winning hands my mother used to draw at the poker tables.

But after a few days with nothing, my mood started turning again. Sure, nothing was happening—nothing might happen until the weekend of the men's retreat. It was the waiting that drove me nuts.

I was starting to feel defeated again. It seemed as if the universe had alerted Ted to my efforts. Once again, I began to think that no one would ever believe me. I began to wonder if Paula still believed me.

I would love to tell you that I am great at planning, but more often than not I do things on the spur of the moment. During one of my occasional moments of strength, I decided on a whim to fire off an e-mail to Patricia Calhoun. She is the editor of *Westword*, a well-known alternative newspaper in Denver. They publish weekly, and they have a reputation for running articles that more mainstream outlets won't touch. The paper had been around since 1977, and I read it every chance I get. *Perhaps they would like this story,* I thought.

I sent her, more or less, the same e-mail I'd sent Paula just a few months earlier. I made sure to stress that I had the voice mail tapes and the envelope he'd sent me, and just to cover my ass, I did not mention Ted Haggard's name anywhere. Once again, I poured my heart out and out it went into the universe.

Naturally, I started daydreaming about telling my story to Patricia. I had seen her on local shows about local issues, and to me, she always stood out as bright and knowledgeable. Since I saw myself as bright and knowledgeable as well, I felt that I knew her and could trust her. Plus, she looked like someone it would be cool to hang out with. Patricia struck me as someone who knocked it around loudly with the best and butchest of them. I hadn't even met her, and suddenly she was my friend.

But to be honest, I felt like I was cheating on Paula. Here I had made a commitment to her, and just because nothing was happening, I'd gone looking for someone else to talk to. I knew that in the real world, you can't play favorites, but one of my biggest strengths—and weaknesses—has always been that I'm very loyal, especially if you show an interest in me. I will be your friend for life as long as you don't screw me over. I felt that Paula liked me, even though I knew she was just doing her job. I didn't want to hurt her. Even though my world was falling apart, I still felt that I had to protect her somehow. No wonder I was a mess.

A few days later, Patricia called me and said she wanted to meet. I was elated to hear from her, convinced that once she heard my story, heard the tapes, and saw the envelope, she would run something. Her phone call helped give me the energy to run some errands and do things that I had post-poned until I was no longer in a crappy mood.

I needed to get my story out there. I was vacillating between going public and staying quiet, so I felt that if I could just get it out there, this inner conflict would end. I still felt guilty about going behind Paula's back, but I didn't want to bring myself down. Once again, I turned to the universe and offered Paula an apology. That made everything better. Maybe the clouds in my life were starting to clear.

Patricia and I scheduled a meeting for Friday morning at eight o'clock sharp. Much like getting ready for a job inter-view, I put on jeans and a shirt and had all my papers prepared in a nice portfolio. I needed to make a good impres-sion. I did not want her to think that I was a street hustler.

She brought me to her office, and I took a seat amid her clutter. Papers and reference materials were scatted all over. It wasn't dirty, just extremely cluttered. Somehow, she seemed to know where everything was. Perhaps it was my gay sensi-bilities, but it was all very unappealing to look at. She needed the *Queer Eye* guys bad.

"Do you feel you are more of a risk taker than, say, a TV station?" I asked her point-blank. After spending more than a month with Channel 9, I was ready for things to move. That morning, I was ready to give her whatever she wanted so my story could get out there.

Patricia confirmed that she was indeed a risk taker. With that, I told her my story. I was very up front with her about my years as an escort and how I had a client who was very well known in religious circles. I told her about the meth. I told her everything. I didn't flinch, and my story was the same one I gave Paula over a month ago. I gave her my real name and my real phone number.

To be sure, Patricia gets dozens of e-mails and phone calls every day. Many of them are from nut jobs, while others are sincere but just don't have any information worth putting into print. Most just need to vent, and *Westword*, for many people, is the perfect place to vent. Nine out of ten stories she chooses to pursue go nowhere. I knew all that and hoped that my story would rise above the rest.

Patricia listened intently. She did not bring other staffers into the meeting like Paula had, and I took that as a good sign. Patricia is the editor, so I figured she'd have the most say about what gets published and what does not.

When I finished speaking, she asked me who this "prominent figure" was. I was hesitant, of course. At that moment, I still felt that I was betraying Paula, and now I felt that I was betraying Ted.

"It's Ted Haggard," I told her.

She either has a great poker face or what I said just was not shocking to her. She did not visibly react, though she did know who Ted Haggard was. Maybe I watch a little too much television, because the one moment of drama I was expecting never happened.

She made a photocopy of the envelope, and I provided her with a copy of the voice mails. As she handed the envelope back to me, I started having more guilty feelings.

"Patty, I am talking with a television station about this," I confessed. "Don't do anything with this just yet, okay?"

Again, either she has a great poker face or what I said was a nonevent. She said yes and didn't flinch. Without saying much more, she thanked me for my time and, well, that was it. She was pleasant, sure, but much like a job interview, I left her office not knowing if I would ever hear from her again.

Once again, I felt defeated. I knew my expectations were

high, but I wasn't prepared to have them shot down so quickly and thoroughly. I knew Paula and Patricia were no strangers to the court system, but it angered me that nowadays everything has to involve lawyers. I knew neither of them were blowing me off, but both clearly felt that something was missing, and apparently the three of us combined couldn't figure out what it was.

Does the public really have the right to know?

This was the question that most concerned Patricia when she thought about my story, I learned from her later. She said she'd found me to be believable. From the first, she found my story interesting enough to schedule our meeting, and afterward she felt our meeting had been worth it. She had done many stories on public figures having affairs, and during the meeting she told me how my story indeed had potential to be something that the public had a right to know about.

But after our meeting, she couldn't quite get her hands around the story. The story was of interest, but not because two men and sex were involved. A decade earlier, if a public figure turned out to be gay, it would be news. Nowadays, if someone turns out to be gay, she told me, "it's not newsworthy at all."

For her, the story wasn't even about the fact that Ted paid me for sex, although that did make the story better. Ted was clearly a national figure, but if the only compelling facts were that he was married and hired a male escort, the story still might not rise to the level of something the public needs to know.

Years earlier, *Westword* had reported a story about then-governor Roy Romer of Colorado and his longtime affair with his former deputy chief of staff. What made the story compelling for Patricia wasn't that it was the governor or that he was having an affair. It was that he was having an affair with someone on his payroll, which was funded by tax dollars.

What made my story fascinating for Patricia was that Ted Haggard had a long history of being antigay and making antigay remarks in public. There were some legal issues involved, but for Patricia, here was a well-known homophobe engaging in homosexual activity, and that was what made it newsworthy.

I was relieved that she saw my story the way I wanted it to be seen. But she still needed more evidence before she could go to press. While she appreciated the voice mail tapes and the envelope, she, like Paula, did not feel that there was enough evidence. She felt that there was still no smoking gun or, in her words, no "smoking penis."

"This is going to be a 'he said, he said,' so you need a credible first 'he said.'" She got that first credible "he said" from me. From that point on, however, it seemed that my story would run out of steam, just like it had with Channel 9. Even if she had everything I'd said vetted and then took it down to Colorado Springs to confront Ted, the story might still go nowhere, she told me. If Ted flat out denied everything, that could stop the story in its tracks. Another possibility, she warned, was that Ted and his handlers could keep putting her off until after the election or longer, effectively killing the story until something else happened. That could go on indefinitely.

Now I was really feeling defeated. Twice up to bat and twice I'd struck out.

I called Patricia a few days later, but no plans were afoot. She was still interested, she assured me, but that's about all she had to say.

I think Patricia would have loved to run with the story, but she ran into some logistical challenges as well. Being a weekly paper, she got only one chance a week to break news. She could break a story online but preferred to put her banner stories in the print edition first. My story clearly could have been a banner story for her.

In another e-mail to her, I asked her again to hold everything until the TV station I was working with made a move. She told me she would not pursue the story until I told her it was okay.

My moods were still all across the board. One minute I was convinced that my story was solid and that I just needed to get it to the right reporter. The next minute I was wallowing in self-pity, convinced that I was dealing with a force larger than life, a man who had all the media, and perhaps even the world itself, in his back pocket. All I could do was curse Ted, but even that did nothing for me.

That afternoon, the sun was shining again. It was a perfect day to go for a walk in the park, so I took a long lunch and saw a client later in the afternoon. I have a friend in Buffalo, New York, whom I had been meaning to see for some time. When I got home, I called him to ask if I could still go see him. He said sure. He was happy that I was coming for a visit. Then I left a message for Patricia, saying I was going out of town for a few days and asking her not to do anything with the story until I got back.

In New York, walking around Niagara Falls, I told my friend in a very roundabout way what was happening. I wished I could have told him that I was an escort and that Ted Haggard was a client—perhaps we could have strategized together—but I didn't. Instead, I told him that if I went through with what I was thinking of doing, he might see me on the national news.

"Really?" my friend replied. "Well, good luck with every-thing."

I started to think about my friendships. Perhaps I needed to tell people who I really was and what I'd been doing for my entire adult life. I was feeling just like I had as a child—alone and of little worth. When I got back to Denver, I could feel my depression start to hit almost the moment I opened the door to my apartment. I called Paula and Patricia just to see where things were. They both asked if Ted had called me, and I told them no. Things were still on for the men's retreat that weekend, but it seemed as if both reporters had lost all interest in me.

The Friday night before the retreat started, an unmarked van parked right outside my apartment building; it would remain there all weekend. Paula told me it was a Channel 9 van and to try to pretend that it wasn't there.

The weekend arrived, and I was full of anticipation. Every time the phone rang, I knew it would be Ted. The phone probably rang about twenty times that weekend and not once was it Ted.

I just didn't understand. It seemed odd that Ted called me more than usual in August and now, when I wanted him to call and to stop by, nothing. Did someone leak information to Ted? Was he out rustling up support for the Colorado antigay marriage amendment?

All weekend long, the van was parked right outside my apartment building. By Sunday afternoon, Ted still hadn't shown up, and I was certain they were calling me a bunch of names, including "liar."

Maybe Ted wasn't coming around because I'd blown him off about getting more meth. Maybe the math was simple: no meth, no sex, no fun for him. His feelings were hurt, and he probably felt that whatever was there for him on an emotional level was gone. Personally, I thought all the drug use was changing him. Drugs and sex were replacing the emotional needs he had. I was sure he'd sought other avenues to obtain meth.

The weekend came and went with no Ted, and I was really feeling down.

Paula called the Monday after the retreat and told me not to get discouraged, but I could see the writing on the wall. It was pretty simple. Channel 9 wanted more evidence. The only way to get more evidence was for me to see Ted again. I could not get more evidence until he called, since I had no way to reach him. Ted wasn't calling. That meant that my story was not moving.

I was raised with the notion that honesty is the best policy. Some have called me naïve, but I still hold to that mantra. That was why I couldn't give up on my story—I just couldn't stomach Ted's dishonesty.

I went back to a stack of Web pages that I had printed out. The *Colorado Springs Gazette* reported, "Ted is a proponent of Yes on Amendment 43 [which would define marriage as a union between a man and a woman] and No on Referendum I [which would have established domestic partnerships in Colorado]."

My stomach sank again. My only way out of this hell was to do something drastic. With the elections just a couple of weeks away, I saw things coming to a head. What scared me was that I also saw myself being right there in the nose of the rocket when it exploded.

CHAPTER 10

EXPOSING TED HAGGARD

⊞

Friday, October 27, 2006

The gym did not open until five in the morning, but I liked to get there about fifteen minutes beforehand to sit in my car, drink my coffee, and listen to the radio. That's been my ritual for most of my life, and it helps me get my day started. If you want to get on my bad side, try stopping me from going to the gym. It truly is my house of worship.

As I worked on my biceps, I kept thinking about my story and whether it was going anywhere. It was less than two weeks from the November 7 congressional elections, and the entire nation could be in for another round of gay bashing and homophobia if the Republicans won again. Sure, the polls were saying they wouldn't win, but remember Florida in 2000 and Ohio in 2004? I didn't trust the polls. I didn't trust the Republicans either, especially now that I knew Ted was one of them.

Driving home, I turned on a talk radio station. I love listening to talk radio, and even though it can be sophomoric, I like the exchange of ideas between ordinary people like me. My favorite morning yakker is Peter Boyles on KHOW. He's been a fixture on Denver radio forever, and I have respect for him because, in my opinion, he's well read and comes across as intelligent. In addition, Peter has always supported gay rights and the right of same-sex couples to marry. What's not to like about that?

"Just let them get married," Peter was saying that morning. I could tell he was a bit frustrated with the ignorance of some callers. Peter was discussing two initiatives that were going before Colorado voters in November. One was Amendment 43, which asked voters to amend Colorado's constitution to limit marriage to the union of a man and a woman. The other was Referendum I, which would make domestic partnerships—including homosexual ones—legal throughout the state. Personally, the right to marry doesn't mean as much to me as other basic rights. That's why it was much more important to me that voters support Referendum I.

As I listened, driving along Cherry Creek, the callers were starting to get under my skin. "Why should they have special rights?" was one frequent question. This longtime antigay rallying cry mislabels equal rights as special rights. I was getting pissed. Would someone tell me how my marriage to another man could possibly affect someone else's marriage?

Some of the callers used the word "fag," and to this day, that word bothers me. I was called that a lot as a child. It's still a derogatory word to me. You still hear people yelling "faggot" from a moving car. The word remains acceptable for most people, and that's just wrong.

One caller was struggling to use a word other than "fag" or "queer." He kept stuttering, and you could tell he just wasn't comfortable with more acceptable words like "gay." How many times do I have to be called a fag or queer bait before people see how hurtful it is? Did anyone ever think that parents of lesbians and gays are listening and shouldn't have to endure such comments about their children? Every time a person makes a remark like that, they aren't just hurting me, they are also hurting my mother and father.

"The sanctity of marriage will be forever ruined," another

caller chimed in. Let's see. Divorce, serial marriages, spousal abuse, child abuse, forty-eight-hour marriages. Let's also throw in shows like *Wife Swap*. Listening to these people, you'd think that the entire civilized world would come crumbling down if two consenting adults of the same sex were allowed to get married and enjoy the happiness and rights that marriage can bring.

Few people know that in a life or death situation, only family members can legally interact with the person whose life is at risk. Legal married spouses are considered family members, but domestic partners are not. That means that my partner, if I had one, would legally have fewer rights to make decisions for me than a second cousin would.

"I am so glad you all have perfect lives!" I yelled at the radio. My anger was building. As I drove along, I even started to feel that if I couldn't be happy, then no one should be happy. That's unusual for me because I'm generally the first to grant that *everyone* is entitled to happiness no matter who they are. I was taken aback by how much all this marriage talk was upsetting me.

"I don't know anyone who is gay," one caller said. *Bullshit. Your life has probably been saved by a "fag," and you didn't know it because that person was forced to keep their sexual preference a secret.* I found the thoughtlessness of some of the callers amazing. All these people who were talking to Peter had no idea what their gay-bashing preachers were doing when no one was looking. I was letting out steam hotter than my hot coffee. The election was less than two weeks away, and all these antigay measures might pass while the progay measures might fail.

And what the hell were Paula and Channel 9 doing with my story? Why did they need evidence from inside my apartment? I was boiling over, and at the same time I was feeling very discouraged. I wasn't sure anything was ever going to happen.

Back at home, wolfing down my usual large breakfast, I found myself chewing with intensity. The last thing I ever wanted to do was draw attention to myself, but I was feeling more and more like I had to. If I didn't say something soon, I was going to tumble back onto my couch and stay there the rest of my life. I had to say something. The question was what.

I took a seat at my computer and tried to check my e-mails, but as I thought more about Peter's morning radio show, I grew angrier. Then I made a split-second decision. I decided I could not waste any more time waiting for Channel 9 and Patricia to gather more evidence. I pulled up the KHOW Web site, found Peter's e-mail address, and banged out the following letter:

> Hey Pete. Big fan, listen to your show on gays. You want a BIG story; I have been a male escort for 20 years. 80% of my clients are married men. The big news is that I see one of the biggest religious guys in the country. The ultimate hypocrisy. You want to talk to me. I am not a weirdo. One other thing, I have been with politicians, pro athletes, lots of clergy, movie stars, I could have ruined many people through the years but it is not my thing. But I have had it with the hypocrisy from Colorado Springs.

Just like my instant decisions to write to Paula and Patricia, I decided that I had to do this. With just one quick click of the mouse and sooner than I could say Referendum I, my e-mail went out into the universe. I couldn't retrieve it if I wanted to. If I were to change my mind, I'd have to do a lot of backpedaling. Don't get me wrong, I wasn't too worried about my decision, but after all I had been through, I found myself not sure of much of anything, including my own judgment.

Just then, the phone rang, and I froze. I nervously picked it up, then sighed a heavy sigh of relief when I saw a 303 area code on my caller ID. I was still living in fear of seeing a 719 area code.

At times, I really wished I could talk to Ted, and at other times, I feared hearing his voice. I really wanted to know how he was doing, but in the same breath, I wanted to rake him over the coals for not telling me who he was and for putting me through all the hell I'd been through.

"Can I come over today at four?" the 303-area-code caller asked.

I wiped my face, said yes, and pressed the red "end" button on my cell phone, my hand shaking the entire time. I massaged my head and face, said a quick prayer to my mother, and started sorting laundry. I was so looking forward to the day when my life would get back to normal and my days would be nothing more than days.

Imagining Peter Boyles, Ted Haggard, his family, and my mother all in the same vision, I had a feeling that things weren't going to be normal for some time.

Tuesday, October 31, 2006

"Is this Mike?" a youthful voice asked.

Oh no! I double-checked my caller ID to make sure he wasn't calling from a 719 phone number. "Who is this?" I asked nervously.

"It's Greg Hollenback at KHOW, Peter Boyles's producer."

Once again, I was both ecstatic and shocked to be called back. I figured I wouldn't be getting a call unless Peter believed me. And just like before, I also feared that now I was going to have to spill my guts.

"Peter would like to have you on the show tomorrow morning," Greg said.

My mind went in a million directions and nowhere all at once. I agreed, but then quickly added, "There are a few things you need to agree to before I come on your show." I just threw that out, spur of the moment, just like my e-mail to Peter. "I will not use any real names. You have to call me something other than Mike, and I do not want Peter to badger me on the air to reveal the other guy's name."

Greg agreed on the spot, adding he would call me a few minutes before six the following morning.

Well, now I'd done it. It was all going to come out. I remember feeling amazingly calm. I'd thought I would be in knots and return to the bad habits that had defined my life for most of 2006. Instead, I felt like a big burden was about to be lifted off my shoulders. Just moments after that call, I started feeling better.

Then I started thinking about all the things that could go wrong. What if no one believed me? What if Peter took pot-shots at me? What would my father think? This could go nowhere, and it could also explode.

That night, as I lay in bed, I tossed and turned. How I wished I could pick up the phone and call my mother like I used to. I could almost hear her say, "Give 'em hell!"

That brought on another round of intense emotions, and I lay awake that night with a bad feeling about what would happen the next day. But I also knew that the wild ride I was about to get on wasn't going to end anytime soon, and like it or not, it was one I'd initiated and that I'd have to ride out alone.

Wednesday, November 1, 2006

I woke up at four, having slept maybe an hour. It felt odd not to be heading out the door to the gym. I got out of bed, ate a piece of fruit, and started clearing my mind.

My phone rang at about 5:15 a.m. Why was Greg calling me so early?

"Mike, it's Patricia Calhoun." Uh oh. I hadn't talked to her since the prior week, and I'd given her no heads-up on what I was doing with Peter.

Patricia told me how the radio station had been teasing my interview all morning long. They weren't naming names, but she'd called Greg at the station to confirm that it was me. Does this woman ever sleep? To my pleasant surprise, Patricia wasn't angry. I told her that I did not know whether I was doing the right thing or not, but that this was something I felt I had to do. In reply, she told me not to name names just yet, and I told her I wouldn't. She then wished me well and hung up.

Waiting for Greg's call, I stayed away from the couch and instead sat upright in a chair, trying to think positive, calming thoughts. Greg was to call me about three minutes before the hour. I had a bottle of water beside me. I had no idea what to expect. I was as ready as I would ever be.

A few minutes before six, my phone rang, and it was Greg.

"I want Peter to call me Paul, and I will not name the pastor," I repeated.

"No problem," Greg assured me. "Are you ready?" I said yes, and Greg put me on hold. Well, here goes.

"I'd like to welcome Paul to the program," Peter said, "and, boy, does he have a story to tell us." Before Peter let me say anything, he read my e-mail on the air.

A million things ran through my mind. I had been telling

this story in my head over and over, and now it seemed odd to be telling it to the world finally. The fact that I was not in the studio made me feel better. In fact, it seemed just like a phone conversation.

Once Peter was done with his initial interview, he made some personal comments. "I think this man is telling us the truth," he told his audience. "That's my gut reaction."

It was so great to finally hear that. My heart soared a thousand feet into the air.

"I think this story has to come, and it has to come quickly," Peter added. "I think this guy has the goods."

But then Peter started taking calls and e-mails, and my soaring heart fell to my feet again.

"Peter, please do not encourage this man."

"Pete, your guest is such a tease. I'll bet he's good at his job."

"He's fishing for a payoff to keep this a secret."

"In my opinion, this dude is nothing more than a fag trying to promote more of his kind."

There were some people who believed and supported me, but most of them felt I was either lying or trying to stir the pot. I felt like crying every time I was called a fag or a prostitute.

During the commercial breaks, Peter spoke with me, giving me encouragement. I wasn't going to hang up on him, but I was feeling battered.

After a break, Peter came back and said, "I have been talking with this man off air, and I think he's sitting on a keg of dynamite."

The calls and e-mails continued. The whole time, I kept watching the clock on my wall. I was so glad to see that it was almost seven o'clock. I was thoroughly exhausted and ready to go to the gym. Then Peter told his audience that he was going to ask me to stick around for another hour.

I was drained and felt trapped, but I thought, *why not?* During a news break at the top of the hour, I told Peter that my client was Ted Haggard.

The name did not immediately register with him, so he pulled up Ted Haggard's name on an Internet search and then printed off some forty pages of information. I had hoped all of this was starting to make sense to him, but I could tell that the logic of it, if there was any, almost didn't matter. The calls and the e-mails kept coming, and that was good for ratings.

The second hour was almost all incoming calls. My guess is that about 80 percent of the callers were against me. Caller after caller seemed not only ill informed, but downright mean-spirited. I kept getting raked over the coals, and finally I said that someday soon those who doubted me would be eating their words. I kept getting egged on to cough up Ted's name, but I held my ground.

By the time eight o'clock rolled around, I could barely move or speak. I felt like I had been beaten up and left for dead, and to be honest, I was angry. No one who called in to Peter's show understood what I was trying to say. After I hung up with Peter, I went to the couch to lie down, but I left the radio on. Lo and behold, the next voice I heard on Peter's show was none other than Patricia Calhoun's.

"He is very compelling," she told Peter's audience, "but it's going to come down to he said, he said." Well, that's exactly what she'd told me in her office. She went on to say that as for the next leg of the story, we'd just have to wait and see what happened next.

I sat there numb. After her interview, Patricia called me to say that she thought I'd done a nice job on the air. I can't begin to tell you how bad I felt. I thanked her and started to apologize profusely for not letting her run with the story. She told me she would have loved to have been the first to break it but that she was supportive and she understood. Speaking of reporters I'd left out in the cold, I needed to call Paula Woodward and let her know what I had done. I owed her an apology as well.

"May I call you back?" she asked when I spoke to her less than an hour later.

I said sure and hung up. I could only imagine the discussions that were taking place inside Paula's newsroom. They had been sitting on the story for months, and now they had been scooped by a talk-show host who I'd e-mailed less than a week earlier. Well, they hadn't been totally scooped. My name and Ted's name still weren't out there.

Unbeknownst to me, Paula was working another source on my story. Through her network of contacts, she'd found a guy who was willing to corroborate my story, but only if Ted denied doing anything and if New Life Church took no action.

Paula called me back before noon. "Mike, I need you to come down to the studio," she said.

I was still drained from Peter's show, but I felt so bad about going behind her back that I was willing to do anything for her. "Can I ask what you want to see me about?"

"I just need to get you on tape." Before I had a chance to think, I said I'd be at the station in thirty minutes.

I walked up to the front desk, and before I could say a word, the receptionist said, "Hi, Mike, I'll call Paula." A young woman escorted me to the room where Paula was. She asked how I was and introduced me to her two assistants.

Everything was calm and friendly. Perhaps a little too calm and friendly. All three were discussing what they should do with my story. I felt like a fifth wheel sitting in on their brainstorming session. After about an hour of their talking to each other and my saying nothing, I began to wonder if, once again, Paula was going to ask me more questions but do nothing with the story.

"I think we're done for now, Mike," Paula finally said. "Thanks for coming to talk to us."

This was getting old, I thought. I gathered my things, and on my way out the door, I told Paula again how sorry I was about not letting her know before I went on the radio.

"I know, Mike," she said. Always the professional, she added, "Thank you again for coming by."

Later in the day, I received another call from Paula. "Can you come back to the studio?" she asked.

I envisioned another meeting like the one that morning, but I still felt I owed her for going to Peter. "Of course I can," I told her. I stopped folding laundry, grabbed a light jacket, and drove down to the Channel 9 studios, which were less than a ten minute drive from my place.

Another woman met me at the front desk and took me back to the studio. This time, out of nowhere, came three or four people who sat me down, hooked me up with a microphone, and brought in a camera. I sat there calmly, but I was getting antsy again. I tried not to think about what they were going to ask me.

The cameraman adjusted his camera and then told the young woman he was rolling.

She leaned into me and spoke slowly. "Are you absolutely positive that the man you had sex with was Ted Haggard?"

What an odd question. I thought I had already answered that for Channel 9 with a very firm yes months before. "Yes," I said as I looked at her.

"Could you tell me that in your own words?" she asked.

Okay. "Yes," I said carefully. "I am absolutely positive that Ted Haggard was the man I had sex with."

"Are you absolutely positive that Ted Haggard was the man with whom you had a three-year affair?" she asked again.

Was there a problem with my first answer? "Yes, I am," I said again, this time more emphatically. *God, what are you trying to get at? Why would I make all this stuff up?*

"Are you positive that Ted Haggard used meth in your presence?"

"Yes," I again said carefully. "I am positive he used meth in my presence."

"And did you sell meth to Ted Haggard?"

"No, I did not sell meth to Ted Haggard."

The woman leaned back in her chair. "Thank you, Mike, we just needed to have confirmation on tape," she said, unclipping the microphone from my shirt. In a flash, everyone left the room, leaving me all alone. Maybe Channel 9 was finally moving on this story.

I got the sense that something was going on in the newsroom. The action seemed more intense than normal. I got excited, thinking that maybe Paula had cornered Ted Haggard, but at the same time I was still sad about it all.

I could also tell that the newsroom staff was not happy with me. They'd had this story for the last few months and had been sitting on it, waiting for something to happen. Then along comes a talk-radio host who, based on just one e-mail, brought me on his show. I wouldn't have been happy either if I were them, but I hoped they could understand where I was coming from. I had to say something or I was going to go nuts.

One woman came in briefly, smiled, and said, "What were you thinking?"

She smiled again and left the room without saying another word.

Now I was starting to get upset. I wanted to remind them that I'd been waiting for them, and waiting, and waiting. *I came into your offices months ago with this story, and now you're upset at me for not waiting even longer?* But I didn't say that. I sat and watched all the excitement. It seemed that they had everyone in the newsroom working on this story, but as best as I could tell, they were getting nowhere with it.

Sitting there with nothing to do, my eyes started to wander. There was a ton of paper and notes all over the desk where I sat. On one notepad facing away from me were some scribbles, and right in the middle of it, in big black letters, were the words "New Life Church." Underneath it was a phone number with a 719 area code.

I don't know what possessed me, but I decided to dial the number.

"Is Ted Haggard there?" I asked.

The church operator put me through to his assistant, who told me that he was busy. "Would you like to leave a message?" she asked politely.

I said no and hung up. That should have been the end of it, but as I looked out into the newsroom, a strange feeling came over me. Sure, I was truly angry with Ted, but I still felt an obligation to Art.

After another twenty minutes, I dialed the New Life number again.

"He is on the other line," the assistant said again. "May I take a message?"

"I'll just call back," I responded, ending the call quickly.

Was someone from Channel 9 already down there talking to him? I wondered.

As the day wore on, I was having second thoughts about my decision to speak out. I was not wavering on exposing Ted Haggard's hypocrisy. But I was starting to wonder if it was worth all the trouble. Honestly, is anything worth all the trouble?

I decided to call New Life Church again, but Ted's assistant gave me the same answer. "I am a close friend of Ted's, and I really need to talk with him," I said. "Is it possible for you to give me his cell phone number?"

To my shock, she gave it to me.

Staring down at the number, I realized that I had no idea what to do with it. When I looked up, I saw everyone in the newsroom still scrambling. *Oh hell*, I thought. Ted's life was about to be ruined, and I owed it to him to say something.

Up until that afternoon in Channel 9, I did not have a number for him. I never did. That's how I protected my clients and myself. I later learned that he had given his phone number to one of the local adult bookstores so they could call him when the items he ordered came in.

Using my right thumb, I punched his number into my cell phone and nervously pushed send. I got a connection, but his phone just kept ringing. Then, all of the sudden, I got his voice mail.

I swallowed hard. I couldn't decide if I should tell him to come clean or to run and hide. "Ted, Art, whatever your name is," I said with an awful lot of intensity, "this is Mike. Listen, the press is at my door, and I really think we need to talk." I spoke out the ten digits of my cell phone number, but hell, he already had that. "Call me!"

After I hung up, I realized that I was acting on impulse, just like I had when I e-mailed Paula, then Patricia, then Peter.

"Mike," a newsroom staffer said, poking her head inside the door. "Would you be willing to go to Colorado Springs with us?" she said.

"Yeah, sure, whatever you guys want," I replied quickly. Sensing my frustration, the young woman closed the door behind her and left me alone again.

A few moments later, the same young woman stuck her head inside the office again. "Not to worry, Mike, you're not going to Colorado Springs." I was still too rattled to respond, but I was relieved that I wouldn't be going.

In came Paula, looking very professional as always. "You can go now, Mike," she said. "Thanks for coming by. We'll call you if we need you."

I was exhausted and confused, unsure of what their next step would be.

Paula added, "We are going down to Colorado Springs to see if we can talk with Reverend Haggard."

"Good luck," I told her. I gathered my things, and on the way out the door, I told her again how sorry I was for going to Peter.

"I know, Mike, thank you."

So, back home I went. I figured I should put a change of clothes and some lunch inside my backpack so that the next time they called I'd at least be cleaner and better fed.

Eating a small salad for dinner, I thought long and hard about what had happened. I just spent an entire day at Channel 9, and there still might not be a story. Right on the table was my portfolio of evidence. The whole thing was driving me nuts.

And yet, at the same time, I was calm. I was concerned, of course, but in the quiet of my home, I felt that I was at peace with the world.

I was enjoying a very relaxing evening, one of only a handful in months, when my phone rang just a few minutes before ten o'clock.

"You're on in two minutes," Paula said. "Sorry I couldn't give you more notice. I'll talk to you later."

I hung up, but still held the phone nervously in my hand as I thought about what was about to play out. That morning, I was just a guy named Paul. That night, the whole world would know that I was Mike Jones, an escort, a sex worker, a call boy. Not only was Paula going to use my real name, but I knew she would name Ted Haggard. I knew that she would tell the world who we were and that we were homosexuals. She'd already been scooped by Peter Boyles on "Paul's" account of the facts, but she wasn't about to let someone else beat her to the bigger story of the real identities of the parties involved.

I took a seat on the couch and turned on Channel 9. There was co-anchor Bob Kendrick with a big breaking news banner running across the screen. It looked like the news had already been running a few minutes. I thought about trying to call my father, but it was too late. What would I tell him?

A picture of Ted Haggard was in the upper right-hand corner of the screen, right next to a picture of me. Right underneath my profile was my name for all the world to see. Monica Lewinsky came to mind.

My "accusations" were presented first, showing a clip of an interview I did in my apartment about two months earlier. Man, I looked terrible!

Next, they showed a clip that was presumably fresh from Colorado Springs, showing Ted talking to a reporter. He stood there plain as day, denying he ever knew "a Mike Jones" and dismissing everything I said as "election-year politics." A moment later, Ted asked the reporter, "Now what did you say his name was again?" He also said he was steady and faithful to his wife and that he had never had gay sex.

I can't begin to tell you how hard it was for me to see all these lies coming from Ted, an alleged man of God, someone who tells millions of people to be honest.

Ted continued talking and denying everything. There he stood, with embarrassing questions being thrown at him like lightning bolts. He handled it all pretty smoothly, but I knew him too well. I could see in his eyes, as they darted from side to side, how uncomfortable he was. I recognized that storm behind his smile. I'd recognize it anywhere, even in the dark. Perhaps the smooth surface was about to crack.

I found it difficult to watch. The story ended by saying that New Life Church was conducting its own investigation into the matter. I clicked off the TV, not wanting to know what else went wrong in the world that day.

Right after the story aired, Paula called me. "There, it's out," she said. I thanked her quickly before she could cut off the connection.

All of a sudden, I froze. Then I started crying. And as quickly as someone could snap their fingers, I felt completely lost and empty again.

I went to the balcony and stepped into the chilly evening air. Looking west, I have a view of downtown Denver and the Rocky Mountains. But I might as well have been looking at four padded walls.

I felt like the whole world had just imploded and no one had noticed. No one was calling. The universe was still.

I felt defeated. The game had barely begun, and already I had been deemed a loser. I wanted to disappear. As I had done so many times before, I knelt in front of my couch and put my elbows on the cushion and cried. And then I prayed. It was the only thing I could do.

It finally hit me that the word "prostitute," which they used repeatedly in the story, was what was really getting me upset. It's one thing to be called a call boy or an escort, but prostitute sounded much worse to me. I felt the world was seeing me as dirty.

My phone rang and broke the silence. "It's Greg from the Peter Boyles show. Can you come to the studio tomorrow morning and be on the show again?"

I scratched my head, wondering if this would be the first of many interviews to come or the last. "Sure, Greg, whatever you want."

"By the way, there may be some reporters waiting for you when you get here."

"Okay, thanks," I said. Greg added that I should park out back and try to get there early.

I hung up, still in tears and half asleep, and dragged myself to bed. *What was happening?* I wondered. Everything was totally out of my hands, and I had no idea in whose hands it was now.

Thursday, November 2, 2006

Better early than late, my parents taught me.

I arrived at the studio around 6:30 a.m. There was Peter, waiting to personally unlock the door and let me in.

"How are you?" he asked. He may not have been sure if I was Paul or Mike.

I said I was fine, but I wasn't. To be honest, I wasn't sure what I was feeling, even after sleeping for close to six hours. Peter showed me the studio, then took me to the control room and introduced me to Greg.

At five minutes before the hour, Greg took me into the studio and had me take a seat at a very cluttered desk with lots of wires and switches and levers. He explained how the talk buttons and headphones worked and pointed out a monitor in front of me that would show the names and questions of the callers.

At seven o'clock on the dot, the show started. *What names were they going to call me today?* I wondered.

Just like at Channel 9, Peter also asked me to confirm that I had had sex with Ted Haggard. A little more chitchat, and it was open season on Mike Jones.

I really don't remember all the comments that people made, and to be honest, I was trying to block them out of my mind. Most of the callers were not in my camp, to be sure, but they weren't in Ted Haggard's camp either. There were a few callers that had good things to say about me, and I thanked them. One caller pointed out that I had not yet proven my case, and that was true.

All in all, I felt I was handling the callers quite well. When I spoke, Peter looked me squarely in the eye the whole time. You can imagine, however, that it got tiring to be called a liar, a manipulator, and a media whore—and those weren't even the rude comments.

Finally, I'd been called a liar one too many times. I blurted out, "I will take a polygraph test if that will make these people happy." Little did I know that in broadcast land, things can happen quicker than you can write a retraction. Without missing a beat, Peter asked, on the air, if there were any polygraphers out there who could give me a test. Right on the air, a test was scheduled. Talk about reality programming. I felt like I was being set up.

Before I left the studio, another talk show dragged me into

their discussion. The callers were about the same as Peter's. They were either for me or against me, and it usually depended on how religious they were. Once that show was over, I gathered my things and left the building through the back door.

On my way home, I called Paula to see if she'd gotten any feedback on the story that aired. There was nothing she could tell me, but I could tell from her voice that something was up.

New Life Church had issued the following press release earlier that morning:

> Community leaders will hold a press conference today at 3PM at the Gazebo at the downtown Pioneer's Museum. Pastors and community leaders will join together to show support for Pastor Ted in light of politically motivated allegations made yesterday. For more information, please contact Jim Banks.

Associate Pastor Rob Brendle added, "This is clearly a political stunt. Ted is the farthest thing from a homosexual as you can get. Trust me."

By midmorning, James Dobson of Focus on the Family, also in Colorado Springs, had issued a statement:

> It is unconscionable that the legitimate news media would report a rumor like this based on nothing but one man's accusation. Ted Haggard is a friend of mine and it appears someone is trying to damage his reputation as a way of influencing the outcome of Tuesday's election—especially the vote on Colorado's marriage-protection amendment—which Ted strongly supports.

Yet shortly after noon, the New Life Church press conference to support Ted had been cancelled.

When I arrived home, I put my things down and dialed my voice mail number. I was dumbfounded to hear that my mailbox was full. I grabbed a piece of paper and a pen and started playing all my messages. Each caller was from a different area code, and they all wanted to talk to me.

To say I was amazed would be an understatement. Reporters, editors, and photographers from all around the world called me. I grabbed a bottle of water and sat down for what I thought would be a couple of hours of returning phone calls and doing interviews. Yet every time I hung up with one person, five more messages would be waiting for me. It was a madhouse, but I'd be lying if I said I wasn't enjoying it.

Suddenly, there was a loud knock on my apartment door. I froze. All I could think of was what Paula said about getting a lawyer because I had engaged in illegal activity. What if it was someone who'd heard me on the radio and wanted to harm me? I got scared, so I stopped returning calls and sat silently for awhile. Soon, the knocking stopped, but I was still scared. I later learned from the cleaning lady that a couple of local reporters had snuck into the building.

I spent the next five hours returning phone calls. It was exciting, in a way. I was talking to people all over the world, and this time none of them were calling me a whore or a prostitute.

I had no food in my refrigerator, and I hadn't eaten all day. I really didn't want to leave my apartment for fear of getting ambushed, but how was I going to eat? I stopped answering the phone, grabbed a coat and my wallet, and slipped out the back door of my apartment building. As I walked from the alley to the grocery store, I could see the press out front waiting for me to appear. It was both exciting and strange. Fortunately, I did not get ambushed while I was picking up skim milk and whole-grain bread.

I returned home again through the back door. One of the messages waiting for me was from Greg to tell me that they had someone lined up who could give me a polygraph test at three that afternoon.

Before long, it was 2:30 p.m., and I was still talking on the phone. My responses to all who called were starting to sound the same—so much so that I thought I might as well make one recording and send it to whoever's interested.

I really did not want to take the polygraph test, but I had painted myself into a corner. I let the phone ring, hopped into the shower, got dressed, and buzzed out the door. On my way out, I was stopped by Dee, the lady who cleans our building.

"Mike, you are quite the celebrity," she told me. "Those reporters asked me what I thought of you, and I said that you were very nice guy who always treats me with respect and brings me Snickers."

I thanked her and ran off to my appointment. I have to tell you that I could talk with some of the most powerful media people in the world, but when someone like Dee tells me that she thinks I'm a nice guy, it means the world to me. That made my day, truly.

"Nice to meet you, Mr. Jones," said the middle-aged man who greeted me. He told me his name was John and that he would be giving me the polygraph test.

A little on the heavy side, John was very cordial and easy to talk to. Then it hit me: I know nothing about this man. What if he's an evangelical and I've just walked into a trap?

He sat me down and started explaining how the test would measure my blood pressure, pulse rate, and other bodily functions. "Above all," he told me, "relax."

Yet just as he was getting his machine set up, his cell phone rang. It was for me. I thought it odd that someone, most likely a reporter, would call me on *his* cell phone. I had turned mine off so I could focus on the test.

"We've got some breaking news from Colorado Springs," said the Channel 9 staffer. "We need you to come to the studio so we can get a response."

"I'll be there right away," I told the woman. In a flash, I told John I had to leave and apologized profusely for walking out.

Driving there, I was puzzled. What could be so important that I had to drop everything and race back to Channel 9? Did Ted spill his guts? Did they fire him? My stomach was suddenly all in knots. This was not what I wanted, I swear.

"Okay, what happened?" I asked when yet another newsroom staffer greeted me in the lobby. She took me back to the newsroom, which was again abuzz with people scurrying back and forth and phones ringing like crazy.

Just like the day before, a lot was happening, but nothing in particular seemed to be in the works. I sat as patiently as I could.

The following news release came across the wire moments after I arrived:

> Reverend Ted Haggard, Senior Pastor of New Life Church, stated today that he could "not continue to minister under the cloud created by the accusations made on Denver talk radio this morning." He therefore placed himself on administrative leave, pending investigation, spiritual counsel, and a decision by the

church's board of overseers. Pastor Haggard said, "I am voluntarily stepping aside from leadership so the overseer process can be allowed to proceed with integrity. I hope to be able to discuss this matter in more detail at a later date. In the interim I will seek both spiritual advice and guidance."

"He resigned! He resigned!" a staffer cheered.

My eyes welled with tears. No one was saying a word to me directly. I felt sick to my stomach.

"How do you feel about Ted Haggard stepping down?" asked the reporter. I felt like I had been coldcocked. I tried to compose myself, dabbing my eyes to make sure they weren't too puffy. I could hear the camera buzzing, laying in wait for my response.

I cleared my throat and said, "I wish the best for Ted." Damn, this was harder than I'd thought it would be. "I hope he looks within himself and finds honesty. I wish the best for him and his family and congregation." After pausing a moment, I said, "I hope that he can return to the church when the time is right and do what he enjoys in life."

Then, with no emotion whatsoever, one person took off my microphone, another shut down the camera and the lights, and another gathered some papers and other items. And they all left me sitting there, alone.

I don't remember saying good-bye to anyone or even seeing anything else happen. I exited the building and went home. Just like that.

Before I even opened my apartment door, I could hear my phone ringing. Simultaneously, my cell phone started ringing as well. The number on my caller ID was from KHOW.

"Mike, we still need you to do the polygraph test," Greg

said. "Can you do it early tomorrow morning at 5:00 a.m. and then come back to the studio to discuss the results?"

"Okay," I told him, in what sounded to me like the voice of defeat.

Then there was a knock at my door. By that point, I was moving like a zombie.

"Who is it?" I asked. So much for a secured building.

"*Denver Post*, Mike. Could we please speak with you?"

"Hang on." I told Greg I would do it. Then I shuffled to the door, unlocked it, and invited the two people—I assumed a reporter and a photographer—inside. I spouted off the same answers I had given all day and posed for a few pictures. All the while, my phone kept ringing off the hook.

How ironic that the one call I decided to take while the *Post* was there came from the other major Denver paper, the *Rocky Mountain News*.

"Can we come over now?"

Well, why not? They were there in a flash, which made me think they had been parked outside my building. I buzzed them up, answered more questions, and tried to look like the hunk next door while fighting off my emotions and fatigue.

"Are you happy he resigned?" I was asked.

"He only temporarily resigned," I replied. "Who knows what will happen tomorrow?" Truer words had never been spoken.

After the reporters left, my phone kept ringing all through the evening. I got calls from news outlets in Germany, Ireland, Australia, and the BBC in London. Somehow, ABC News got through. They wanted to tape something for their morning show, *Good Morning America*, and asked if they could send a limo for me. I looked at the clock and saw that it was only seven. It felt like it was already well past midnight.

Again, I said sure. The limo picked me up and took me to a studio just west of downtown Denver. I was still wearing the same clothes I'd had on all day. Stopping in front of the building, the driver passed me off to someone who walked me down a long hallway to where two men with a camera and microphone were waiting. By that point, I knew how to slip the microphone wire under my shirt, so I just did it myself.

As I sat in the hot seat, I could hear the two men talking with New York, trying to make sure all communications were working. Then, 3-2-1 and it was show time.

"You're sure it was Reverend Ted Haggard?" they asked. This was getting old. I offered them the tapes I had made of Ted's voice mail messages. A reporter in New York asked one of the men in Denver to get a player so he could listen to them. Apparently, this reporter had interviewed Ted Haggard just a couple of weeks earlier. I started playing the tapes, and as soon as I finished the first one, the reporter said firmly, "That's him, no doubt that it's his voice." That made me feel great because I was still dealing with people doubting my story. Once the question and answer session was done, I posed for some footage, and then, quick as a wink, I was back in the limo and returned to my apartment.

It was almost nine o'clock. The calls started to slow down a bit but not for long. Flashing through the caller IDs, I was impressed by the numbers I saw. Yet after more than twelve hours of nonstop calls to discuss the link between Ted and me, I was getting very tired and feeling more than a little overwhelmed.

Why am I doing this all by myself, I thought. *There must be someone I know out there who can help me.* But try as I might, I couldn't think of anyone I knew whom I could call for help. I knew nothing about the media, but there I was, talking with the Associated Press, *Newsweek, Time*. Even Arianna Huffington called, though she wanted to know more about the nude photo spread I'd done for *Inches* magazine years ago. How did she find out about that?

Before long, it was 10:30 p.m. I had not eaten since morning. Since I usually consume large amounts of food on a daily basis, I was famished by that point. I hadn't had so much as a protein bar all day. My body felt like it was crashing, but there was no way I could fall asleep. I do not sleep very well when my life is boring, and it turns out that I sleep even less well when it seems that everyone in the world wants to talk to me.

Half an hour later, the calls were still rolling in. That night I learned the hard way that many reporters never give up. No one wants to be left out, so they just keep calling.

"No, I did not fall in love with Ted," I told one reporter. As the night wore on, I kept thinking that I had to get to bed so I could take that polygraph test in the morning. I finally managed to turn off my phone around one o'clock.

That night, Ross Parsley, who was quickly appointed interim senior pastor of New Life Church, wrote to the congregation: "It is important for you to know that [Ted] confessed to the overseers that some of the accusations against him are true. He has willingly and humbly submitted to the authority of the board of overseers, and will remain on administrative leave during the course of the investigation." Parsley added, "Please continue to keep Ted and Gayle and their family in your prayers."

Boy, what a long day. As I was finally falling asleep, I realized that no one was coming out of this a winner, including me.

Friday, November 3, 2006

For three days, I had awoken earlier than normal and did not have time to go to the gym. Call me names, but keep me from the gym, and I can get mean. Just in time for my polygraph test, I awoke from a very disturbing nightmare with one very bad migraine. I took a Maxalt tablet and hoped it would kick in fast. On top of that, I was also having trouble breathing, which usually means that an asthma attack is coming on. I reached for my Albuterol inhaler and took a couple of puffs. I wondered if the medication would affect the polygraph results.

John, the polygrapher, met me at the door of his office and took me to the room where he had his equipment set up. More nervous than the previous day, I asked him if my migraine and wheezing and overall queasiness would affect the polygraph test.

"It shouldn't," he replied.

We spent almost an hour going over questions and procedures. He asked me if I understood everything. I felt I did, so we started the test.

None of his questions were about drugs. The first one was simple: "Did you have sex with Ted Haggard." Of course my answer was yes.

It was impossible to feel relaxed with all those wires hooked up to your arms and chest.

Another question he asked was, "Have you ever sneaked a peek at another man at a urinal?" I would have responded yes, but he had prepped me earlier to answer no on that question. My guess is that he needed that to make sure a lie would show up on his monitor.

After he was done, I was ready to thank him and leave. But then he said that we were going to do it all over again, just to make sure the results from the first round of questions did not vary. I was not happy, but I had come this far, so I said sure.

After he got his last reading almost thirty minutes later, I was glad to get unhooked from all the equipment. While I waited, John pulled out the printout of the test and examined it. I watched him mark certain areas and write some comments. It was nervewracking, but I felt fine because I was sure everything was all right, and it would show I was truthful.

After checking a few more things, John looked at me sternly and said, "Mike, I have some bad news. Your test shows deception."

"What?" I exclaimed. "Are you kidding?" Suddenly, I felt I was being set up, but I knew I had to keep calm. "What is 'deception'?" I asked as calmly as I could.

John told me that rather than say someone "failed" a polygraph test, which is technically incorrect, the results of a polygraph may indicate that someone is trying to deceive or not present a correct or honest picture. He also told me that people who give polygraphs do not use the words "lying" or "liar."

John went on to say that the polygraph simply showed "deception," repeating that word again. But to me, that meant I was a liar. And now this information would be made public, and everyone would think I'd made the whole story up.

I was devastated. I sat there, slumped in my chair. I called Peter to let him know the horrible news.

"You haven't been lying to me, have you?"

Peter's response to my "deception" was pretty flat, and the thought of taking more angry calls from listeners plunged me into an even worse mood. I gathered my things, hopped in my Pontiac, and began one of the longest thirty-minute drives of my life, all with John right on my tail since he was going to be on the show as well.

"It's all over!" I said to myself. Once again, I cried. How would I dispute the test? How was I going to face Peter, Paula, Patricia, the reporters, and the public? All I could envision was a big headline that read "LIAR," right next to a picture of a smiling Ted Haggard.

I took some deep breaths and reminded myself that I am a survivor. I have survived everything from bullying to baseball bats to the head. I would survive this, too.

Did you have sex with Ted Haggard? Are you absolutely sure?

How could I have failed? I asked myself. As I came within blocks of the studio, I tried to steer my mind toward happier thoughts. I did not want anyone to see me cry. To make matters worse, several television trucks with high antennas protruding into the sky were parked in front of the radio station waiting for me. I drove right past them and parked in the back as I had before.

A staffer met me at the back door and let me in. Instantly, my public relations persona went into action. I wore the same game face I used when a client arrived for an appointment. It had served me well throughout my life, but this was the first time I remember questioning whether or not my face would hold up.

When the elevator stopped at the studio floor, I felt my heart sink all the way back to the ground floor. The doors opened, and the games began. It was Mike Jones versus the world this time.

I mustered a smile, trying to hide my pain. None of the photographers and reporters heckled me, and they all seemed nice. There must have been ten to fifteen of them.

Once I got inside the KHOW studio, I sat down, put on a pair of headsets, and waited for the show—or the roast—to begin. Five cameras and reporters also crowded in with me, as well as John, the polygrapher, and Peter. The whole time, I held on to my portfolio, the one with the envelope from Art, my tapes of his voice mail, and other items that would help me prove my case.

As the show started, Peter told the world that he would be reading the results of my polygraph test live on the air. *Where would it all end?* I wondered.

After a commercial, Peter asked John for the results, and my mind went blank.

"The test showed deception," John said. By that point, I had given up trying to keep my poker face on.

"I must admit, I was surprised by the results," John added.

He went on to say that, based on his preliminary interview with me, I seemed to be telling the truth. I tried to listen more closely, but my migraine was going so strong that I could hear my own heartbeat better than I could hear John and Peter.

"What do you think, Mike?" Peter asked me.

"I just don't get it," I said. "The questions were about sex, not drugs. Sex is the reason Ted Haggard contacted me to begin with." I took a deep breath, trying to remember what I just said and searching for my next words. "I stand by my story and the facts."

"I'd like Mike to take the test again when he isn't so tired," John added.

John's comments made me feel somewhat better, but I was still a train wreck. Fortunately, I did not have to take any calls from listeners that day. If I had to be called a liar and a dirty whore and a goddamn fag all in one morning, it might as well have been the end of whatever this circus was.

By the end of the hour, all I wanted to do was leave, but the mob of reporters was still there, laying in wait. These were hardworking people who are just doing their jobs, so I stayed and talked with everyone.

"We understand you failed the polygraph test. Do you have any comment?" This was a common question.

I gave them the same answer I gave Peter. I took other questions and tried to smile. I stayed about another hour talking to reporters, including going back into the building to do another interview with one of the FM stations. Even as I did all this, I feared that the next morning I would see a banner headline that read "Mike Jones is a liar."

At about nine o'clock, I was done, and I wanted to get home. Actually, what I really wanted to do was start over, but I knew I couldn't. I hadn't eaten, I hadn't slept, I was still having trouble breathing. I was a wreck, but I didn't think it was showing.

Another radio staffer escorted me to my car, and I drove off. No one was following me, and I even had mixed emotions about that. It was not a fun drive home. I was already sick and depressed, and then, just like the night before, my cell phone started ringing.

Did I really want to answer it? What did I have to say that I hadn't said already? One time I saw that it was Paula calling, and I definitely wanted to talk to her.

"How are you, Mike?" she asked in a very sincere tone. "Are you okay?"

I spilled my guts to her and started crying. I was so desperate for someone to listen to me.

"Everything will be okay, Mike," she assured me. "We are having a voice expert listen to your tapes."

"Really?" I said with excitement. "What did he say?"

"I'll tell you more later, Mike. Everything will be okay. I just wanted to make sure that you're all right."

Before I knew it, she had hung up. She was like that. She'd say what she needed to say and then be gone. Well, at least I got to talk with her.

Her call did make me feel better. If they can match Ted's voice with the voice on the tapes, then everyone will know that I was telling the truth. Right?

I still felt like crap when I got home, only to find my picture on the morning newspaper staring right back at me. "Revelation: Male escort states he had sex with evangelist." I guess I was feeling better because all I could see was how bad my face looked. Yet rather than go back to bed, I decided to sit and return phone calls. Once again, it was quite an impressive list of callers from all over the world.

I was trying to prioritize. MSNBC asked me to do a live interview at noon. "Sure, I'll be ready when the limo arrives," I told the woman who called. That made me feel better. If they're still sending limos, they must not think I'm a liar. Right?

Moments later, the interview with Ted Haggard that would prove me correct aired on Channel 9's noon newscast:

CHANNEL 9: Have you used meth?

TED: No, I have not.

CHANNEL 9: Okay, and the voice expert that is in Denver that was hired by KUSA has . . . matched now eighteen of the words left on the voice-mail message.

TED: Yes. I did call him. I did call him.

CHANNEL 9: And what did you call him about?

TED: I called him to buy some meth, but I threw it away.

CHANNEL 9: And who were you buying the meth for?

TED: No one. I was buying it for me, but I never used it.

CHANNEL 9: Have you ever used meth before?

TED: No, I have not. And I did not ever use it with him.

CHANNEL 9: And did you ever have sex with him?

TED: No, I did not.

CHANNEL 9: And at what point did you decide to throw away the meth?

TED: Right after. I never kept it very long because it's . . . it was wrong. I was tempted. I bought it. But I never used it.

CHANNEL 9: And how did you know that he would sell it to you?

TED: He told me about it. I went there for . . . I went there for a massage. So, okay, we're late for our appointment. And so . . . but thank you for your work.

CHANNEL 9: How did you find him to get a massage from him?

TED: A referral.

CHANNEL 9: From?

TED: From the hotel I was staying at.

CHANNEL 9: The hotel where?

TED: I stay at a lot of hotels in Denver because I write in Denver.

After that clip ran on Channel 9, news outlets throughout the world picked it up and ran it, usually unedited.

My driver took me to a nondescript building in downtown Denver. You would never know it was a television studio from the outside. I hung out for about ten minutes, used the restroom, drank some water, and made sure my hair looked all right. Then it was show time at 12:30 p.m.

Rita Cosby was my first national live interview, and to my surprise, I wasn't very nervous about it. There wasn't any noise or other people in the studio, so it almost seemed like I was talking to myself. I took a deep breath, asked my mother for help, and watched the show start.

Then out of nowhere came Rita's voice. One of the studio guys pointed at the camera, signaling me to just talk to the camera. I might have felt uncomfortable, not being able to see what was happening, but that afternoon this was the closest I got to relaxation.

Rita first talked about Ted's just-released comments: the meth, the massage, and so on. "What do you think?" she asked me.

At that moment, I had not yet seen the tape of him talking from his SUV. "That reminds me of . . . Clinton—I smoked but I didn't inhale," I replied. Not my best answer, but I was trying to show that Ted's answer sounded more like denial than truth.

She also asked me about Ted's assertion that I sold him meth. Here, I had to make my case and hammer away at it.

"I never sold him the meth," I proclaimed. "He contacted me three years ago, as an escort. He asked me, 'What do you know about meth? I've always been curious about it, do you think you can get me some?'" I was prepared for that question, so I made sure that my side of the story got out fast and hard. I also told her that Ted did some meth each time before we got naked.

"So would it be accurate to say that you're alleging, what, more than a dozen times you saw him snort?" she asked, rather pointedly.

"Yes," I replied.

"For sure?" she asked.

"Yes," I said again. I was beginning to understand why reporters were asking me these questions over and over again. If I were in their shoes, I, too, would want to be absolutely sure that this escort's story didn't change.

"Do you have any proof that he actually paid for sex, that he actually hired a prostitute?" she asked.

I told her no, I did not have any proof. There were no cancelled checks or receipts, and I certainly wasn't going to show her my bank statements. I went on to tell her about the envelope that was mailed from Colorado Springs and how it contained two hundred-dollar bills.

Then she asked me to show the envelope to the audience, and I did. There was an incredible glare from the studio lights that blinded me.

"You know Reverend Haggard is married and has five kids," she said and then asked what Ted and I discussed about his personal life during our sessions. I told her that we never discussed his personal life, though he did tell me that he was married.

"There were no emotions in this relationship at all. It was strictly business," I asserted.

"Strictly sex?"

"Strictly sex." I went on to say how he normally paid me two hundred dollars a visit and that our visits suddenly ended in August for no apparent reason. She pushed me a bit, and I said I was probably paid two hundred dollars every month for three years, which comes to about seventy-six hundred dollars in total.

"What other evidence do you have?"

I told her about the two voice mails.

"Why are you revealing this now?" she asked pointedly. "A lot of people are wondering what's up with the timing."

I told her truthfully that I did this right before the election because I was upset about the proposed amendment to the Colorado constitution that would limit marriage to the union of a man and a woman.

"Were you ever paid off? Did any political party get to you?"

"I made this decision myself," I insisted.

"You failed a lie detector test this morning. Why do you think you failed?" Before I had a chance to respond, she threw in, "Why should we believe you?"

I told her, just as I told Peter's audience earlier that morning, that I don't know why I failed the test. Still, I was calm talking to Rita, perhaps too calm.

I knew she was wrapping up when she asked, "If Reverend Haggard is watching right now, what do you want to say to him?"

"I want to tell him that I'm really sorry that he's in the position he's in. You know, what this proves is we are all human, we are all sinners. But when you're in a position of authority and a role model for millions of people, you really need to practice what you preach. And I hope that after this passes he can continue in the church if that's what he chooses. And I wish the best for him . . ."

"This could be criminal activity, hiring an escort. Are you planning to go to the authorities? My final question to you."

"I am not."

"What if they ask for it? Will you hand over whatever you have?"

"Sure," I told her, "if I am forced to do so." Quick as a wink, she said thanks and I said thanks and it was over.

Some friends have since commented that I should have smiled more and been more lively. You have to remember that as far as I was concerned, there was nothing to smile about. I was not happy about anything that had happened, including Ted losing his position as president and his pastorship. I feared that if I smiled or came off as lighthearted, I would have been seen as suspect. What is surprising to me is how well I did on almost no sleep in two days.

I had barely unhooked my microphone when someone asked me if I could stay seated for another interview on MSNBC, this time with Tucker Carlson. I figured why not and remained seated right where I was.

Tucker started the interview with some incorrect information.

"[Ted] had a three-year relationship with a gay prostitute called Mike Jones, who worked for a company called Rent-Boy.com."

I never worked for RentBoy.com. Who told him that? I had advertised there, which must be what had caused the confusion.

"Jones says he had sex with Haggard once a month over that period, sex Jones described as 'vanilla.'" He then played the Channel 9 tape. I found it fascinating. That was the first time I had heard Ted talk about what happened.

"You heard the Reverend Haggard describe the massage that took place between you. You described what took place as 'vanilla' sex. Could it be you are talking about the same thing?"

"No, I mean, massage is not sex."

"So you are maintaining that without question there was sexual activity between you, there's no mistaking it, you two had sex?"

"Absolutely."

"So . . . you believe the Reverend Haggard is lying?"

I had to repeat myself a lot on this question, but it was important. If I didn't come right out and say Ted was lying, it would have made me seem ambiguous, and everyone would have jumped all over that. I had to say again that Ted was lying when he said a hotel had referred him to me. "No concierge in Denver would have referred me."

We talked about Ted's mode of transportation. I said I had observed him driving an SUV during the winter and a motorcycle during the warmer months.

"And, of course, he was famous for riding a motorcycle, Mr. Haggard was," Tucker added.

"I didn't know that," I replied.

I was again asked about selling meth to Ted, and I denied it again, emphatically.

"So why was he sending you the money for the crystal meth?"

"Apparently, he couldn't get any on his own, and he was, I guess, hoping that I could find someone to get some for him." So far, so good, I felt.

"Why did you decide to go public with this?"

Nice softball, Tucker. "The more I investigated and looked into his church and his teachings, I just thought, you know what? This is so hypocritical. How dare he say it's wrong for homosexuals to be able to have marriage with their partner, as consenting adults, whom they love, and he can go behind his wife's back and have gay sex? That is just hypocritical."

"Yes. Well, I mean, it is hypocritical. Of course, you're absolutely right." Wow, this was as good as it gets. "[Ted has], I suppose, destroyed his own life, but you've made it possible. And, you know, he has five children." *So it's my fault he and his wife have five children who are now hurting?* Tucker asked me, just like everyone else had, if I had thought about calling Ted to discuss all this first. I told him I had. I said again that I had no help and made the decision to proceed totally on my own.

Tucker was a bit more pointed when he asked me about failing the polygraph test. "People typically don't, as you know, fail these if they are telling the truth. Were you lying about anything?"

"No, I was not lying."

This was going much smoother than Rita's interview, and he was freely telling his audience what he thought of me, so even better. "Yes, I mean, you are a gay prostitute, and he admits he went to you. So kind of 'case closed' as far as I'm concerned, but it is sort of weird that you failed."

After he ended the interview with me, he talked with an evangelical pastor about why homosexuality is so important to them. Tucker said how he first felt sorry for Ted, but after Ted did an interview in his car with his wife and three of his kids, "[he] decided he's a pig. Anybody who would use his family at a time like this, bringing further shame and humiliation upon them is beneath contempt."

The guest reverend went on to urge Ted to "come clean," adding that "the gospel is as sharp as a two-edged sword."

On the way home, the limo driver told me he'd watched me on the monitor, and he thought I'd done well. That made me feel very good.

I got home and the phone calls kept coming, but that may have been because my voice mail box was full. By chance, one of the calls I took was from NBC's *Today Show*. They wanted me to appear on their Saturday program and offered me a flight and hotel accommodations. I have to admit that I was flattered by the offer. I was getting the sense that maybe the world really did want to hear my story. How could I not be excited—and feel better about myself?

After saying yes, they called back fifteen minutes later with my flight information and to tell me that a limo was coming in thirty minutes to pick me up.

You could hear me scream as far away as New Life Church. I wasn't screaming with joy but with panic, because right in the middle of everything, I now had to pack and quickly leave town, something I wasn't sure I should be doing right at that moment.

I went into a frenzy. I laid out a suitcase and started throwing all kinds of things in it. I was so tired, and my brain was fried. I don't remember what I packed, but I hoped I would not forget something important, like my migraine medicine.

The limo arrived, I grabbed my suitcase, and the phone was still ringing. By the time I got to my hotel in New York, it was almost one in the morning eastern time. NBC put me up at the Waldorf-Astoria with a few hundred dollars of room service. I was starved, so I ordered about seventy-five dollars in food that night. As I ate, I tried to check messages on my home phone's voice mail. Before going to bed, I took one of the nicest showers I have ever taken, and it felt good. Maybe I had made the right decision after all.

Saturday, November 6, 2006

It was not long before my wake-up call at five in the morning, leaving me with just three hours of sleep. I ordered eggs and oatmeal, ate, and got dressed, stopping just long enough to check in with my mother to see if I was still doing the right thing.

On the set of the *Today Show*, everyone was nice, but it felt weird being interviewed while everyone on the street could stare through the window in front of me. I kept being pulled in and out of the green room for segment teasers for my upcoming interview with Lester Holt.

It went quickly, and soon I was back at the hotel. I had a radio interview for about thirty minutes. Then it was time to pack again. The requests for interviews still kept coming, including *People* magazine and *The Advocate*. I told them I would call them when I got back to Denver.

While I was on the plane, New Life Church issued this release:

> We, the Overseer Board of New Life Church, have concluded our deliberations concerning the moral failings of Pastor Ted Haggard. Our investigation and Pastor Haggard's public statements have proven without a doubt that he has committed sexually immoral conduct.
>
> The language of our church bylaws state that as Overseers we must decide in cases where the Senior Pastor has "demonstrated immoral conduct" whether we must "remove the pastor from his position or to discipline him in any way they deem necessary."
>
> In consultation with leading evangelicals and experts familiar with the type of behavior Pastor Haggard has demonstrated, we have decided that the most

positive and productive direction for our church is his dismissal and removal.

In addition, the Overseers will continue to explore the depth of Pastor Haggard's offense so that a plan of healing and restoration can begin.

Pastor Haggard and his wife have been informed of this decision. They have agreed as well that he should be dismissed and that a new pastor for New Life Church should be selected according to the rules of replacement in the bylaws.

That process will begin immediately in hopes that a new pastor can be confirmed by the end of the year 2006. In the interim, Ross Parsley will function as the leader of the church with full support of the Overseers.

A letter of explanation and apology by Pastor Haggard as well as a word of encouragement from Gayle Haggard will be read in the 9:00 and 11:00 service of New Life Church.

Paula called me when I was on my way home from Denver International Airport to tell me what had happened.

"You mean they fired him?" I asked her.

She confirmed this, and I lost it right there in the limo. In the past seventy-two hours, I'd had little rest, been called names, failed a polygraph test, and it was simply overwhelming for me. To hear that Ted had been removed from New Life Church created additional guilt for me. I felt this mess was all my fault.

I still had Paula on the line. She patiently waited until I was a bit more composed, then she told me that Ted was going to address the members of New Life Church the following day at the Sunday service.

"He's going to speak to them? In person?"

"We don't know," Paula said. Her careful way of saying things was starting to wear me out, even though I understood why she was like that.

I wondered what he might say. Was there going to be any reference to me? And if there was, would he be apologetic or vengeful? Was he going to call me a dirty lying whore?

By the time the limo pulled up to my apartment, it already felt like a month had passed. In less than a week, the whole world knew my tale of sex for sale and my client's meth use and the pastor with the big smile.

Even worse, the whole world knew that I was forty-nine, just one year away from being eligible for membership in AARP. Most people think I'm much younger, so some friends asked me why I gave out my real age. Like I could hide that from the press!

I had scheduled three or four radio interviews for that night and more the following day. I had little sticky notes plastered all over the walls, reminding me of when someone was supposed to call for an interview. Some ten different gay media outlets were trying to get my attention, too. Maybe I just can't say no to anyone if they treat me nicely. I also enjoyed the attention, to be honest.

But it was starting to overwhelm me. Some guidance and support would have meant so much to me. I thought that perhaps a media person from a gay organization would have contacted me now that I'd single-handedly brought down one of the most powerful gay bashers in the country. Well, I had started all this on my own, and it looked like I'd have to finish it on my own.

Sure, I'll do an interview. No, I did not sell him meth. Yes, I had sex with Ted Haggard. Why would I lie about that? Yes,

Mike Jones is my real name. No, I don't have a partner. Did I forget to tell them that my mother was Shirley Jones?

"Mike, can you do another live interview with Rita Cosby?" the caller asked. Before I could say no, the caller said a limo would be at my apartment building at 8:30 the next morning. Just then, I looked at the clock and noticed that it was almost midnight. I had been up for almost twenty-one hours straight. As much as I hated to, I decided to take a sleeping pill and hope that I didn't wake up with a migraine.

Sunday November 5, 2006

Even with the sleeping pill, I still woke up around five o'clock. How odd that on this big day for New Life Church, my phone was not ringing. I figured everyone was waiting for Ted's letter. Thank God I was not, for a change, the center of this media circus.

I took the opportunity to check my e-mails, the first time in days, and, wow, there were hundreds. People had found my old Web sites and sent messages. The messages came from gays, straights, married people, singles. Some were hateful and a few were rather threatening, but most were supportive of me. These letters of support raised my spirits tremendously. In fact, I printed a few of them and pasted them around the house to cheer me up.

I showered and got ready for Rita Cosby. It seemed that she was trying to time her interview with me with the reading of Ted's letter to his congregation.

The whole world stood still, it seemed, when a gentleman approached the lectern at New Life Church and read Ted's final words as Pastor.

My Dear New Life Church Family,

I am so sorry. I am sorry for the disappointment, the betrayal, and the hurt. I am sorry for the horrible example I have set for you.

I have an overwhelming, all-consuming sadness in my heart for the pain that you and I and my family have experienced over the past few days. I am so sorry for the circumstances that have caused shame and embarrassment to all of you.

I asked that this note be read to you this morning so I could clarify my heart's condition to you. The last four days have been so difficult for me, my family and all of you, and I have further confused the situation with some of the things I've said during interviews with reporters who would catch me coming or going from my home. But I alone am responsible for the confusion caused by my inconsistent statements. The fact is, I am guilty of sexual immorality, and I take responsibility for the entire problem.

I am a deceiver and a liar. There is a part of my life that is so repulsive and dark that I've been warring against it all of my adult life. For extended periods of time, I would enjoy victory and rejoice in freedom. Then, from time to time, the dirt that I thought was gone would resurface, and I would find myself thinking thoughts and experiencing desires that were contrary to everything I believe and teach.

Through the years, I've sought assistance in a variety of ways, with none of them proving to be effective in me. Then, because of pride, I began deceiving those I love the most because I didn't want to hurt or disappoint them.

The public person I was wasn't a lie; it was just incomplete. When I stopped communicating about my problems, the darkness increased and finally dominated me. As a result, I did things that were contrary to everything I believe.

The accusations that have been leveled against me are not all true, but enough of them are true that I have been appropriately and lovingly removed from ministry. Our church's overseers have required me to submit to the oversight of Dr. James Dobson, Pastor Jack Hayford, and Pastor Tommy Barnett. Those men will perform a thorough analysis of my mental, spiritual, emotional, and physical life. They will guide me through a program with the goal of healing and restoration for my life, my marriage, and my family.

I created this entire situation. The things I did opened the door for additional allegations. But I am responsible; I alone need to be disciplined and corrected. An example must be set.

It is important that you know how much I love and appreciate my wife, Gayle. What I did should never reflect in a negative way on her relationship with me. She has been and continues to be incredible. The problem was not with her, my children, or any of you. It was created 100% by me.

I have been permanently removed from the office of Senior Pastor of New Life Church. Until a new senior pastor is chosen, our Associate Senior Pastor, Ross Parsley, will assume all of the responsibilities of the office. On the day he accepted this new role, he and his wife, Aimee, had a new baby boy. A new life in the midst of this circumstance—I consider that confluence of events to be prophetic. Please commit to join with Pastor Ross and the others in church leadership to make their service to you easy and without burden. They are fine leaders. You are blessed.

I appreciate your loving and forgiving nature, and I humbly ask you to do a few things:

Please stay faithful to God through service and giving.
Please forgive me. I am so embarrassed and ashamed. I

*caused this and I have no excuse. I am a sinner. I
have fallen. I desperately need to be forgiven and
healed.*

*Please forgive my accuser. He is revealing the decep-
tion and sensuality that was in my life. Those sins,
and others, need to be dealt with harshly. So, forgive
him and, actually, thank God for him. I am trusting
that his actions will make me, my wife and family,
and ultimately all of you, stronger. He didn't violate
you; I did.*

*Please stay faithful to each other. Perform your func-
tions well. Encourage each other and rejoice in
God's faithfulness. Our church body is a beautiful
body, and like every family, our strength is tested
and proven in the midst of adversity. Because of the
negative publicity I've created with my foolishness,
we can now demonstrate to the world how our sick
and wounded can be healed, and how even disappointed and betrayed church bodies can prosper
and rejoice.*

*Gayle and I need to be gone for a while. We will never
return to a leadership role at New Life Church. In our hearts,
we will always be members of this body. We love you as our
family. I know this situation will put you to the test. I'm sorry
I've created the test, but please rise to this challenge and
demonstrate the incredible grace that is available to all of us.*

Ted Haggard

What a well-written letter, I thought. It certainly pulled at
the heartstrings, as was evident by all the crying and all the
tissues being passed around inside the church.

Yet the more I thought about the letter, the more hollow it sounded. Where were the specifics? He used words like "dirty" and "dark." What the hell did that mean?

I was grateful that he asked the congregation to "forgive [his] accuser" and "thank him." But why did I need forgiveness? Were people supposed to forgive me for being gay? For being an escort? For being honest?

I would have preferred if Ted had said, "Please forgive my hypocrisy. Mike was right. If two consenting adults who love each other, who want to share a life and grow old together want to get married, they should have that right with no exceptions."

AFTER TED RESIGNED

⊡

Election day 2006 was just two days after Ted's letter was read to the New Life congregation. Denver was having a major problem with their voting machines, and I wound up spending three hours in line waiting to vote.

Fewer voters appeared to have cast votes based on so-called morals issues, such as same-sex marriage, than they did two years before in 2004. Colorado had two initiatives on the ballot in 2006. The effort to change the Colorado constitution to limit marriage to a man and a woman passed, and an effort to legalize domestic partnerships failed. Because of what I did just days before the election, many people, including many gays, blamed me for the outcome of those ballot initiatives. That's impossible. The votes weren't even close on both issues, so to blame someone like me is nothing short of scapegoating. Ironically, the same people who blamed me didn't give me any credit for helping the Democrats return to power, including the Democrat who was elected governor of Colorado.

After Ted resigned and left town for reparative therapy, or whatever it was he was doing, I still found myself in the spotlight. Media outlets like CNN and *People* magazine all wanted to interview me. I was determined to talk with everyone who asked, no matter how large or small their audience. Even at the polls, people wanted to talk with me, and I wanted to ensure that we had time for discussion.

I spent election night in Colorado Springs. A local radio station wanted me on the air the next morning, so they put me up at a hotel. When I checked in, the clerk asked me if I was "the" Mike Jones. I said, "That depends." I was still feeling defensive, and I was in Ted Haggard's backyard. The clerk went on to tell me that he was a member of New Life Church, and he thanked me for what I did. I graciously accepted his thanks, shook his hand, and went to my room to rest.

Even in Colorado Springs, the overwhelming majority of people I spoke with were supportive of what I did. Many members of New Life called the radio station the following morning when I was doing the live show. I found it odd that they were thanking me for exposing Ted Haggard. One minute they believe everything he says, and the next minute they want nothing to do with him. Still, their comments to me were sincere, and even my critics were almost all courteous and thoughtful. Some even invited me to come down to New Life Church, promising that my reception would be warm.

A couple of months before the election, a documentary called *Jesus Camp* opened in theaters across the country. Ted Haggard was featured prominently, pointing to the camera and saying his now-infamous line: "I think I know what you did last night. If you send me a thousand dollars, I won't tell your wife." When the DVD was released in January 2007, it contained extra footage of Ted Haggard. The movie was nominated for an Academy Award for Best Documentary Feature. It's a good documentary, and I was proud to have helped it get a wider audience.

Naturally, I did get some troubling calls on my home phone:

"You will not live to see tomorrow."

"Hey Punk, you made a big, big mistake."

"You live in Capitol Hill of Denver, and me and my friends want to meet you [and] play a little baseball. You just show up, and we'll bring the bats."

But I also got an overwhelming amount of wonderful e-mails:

Judy in North Carolina wrote, "You're our hero. If I were your mother, I would be so proud of you. Heck, I am anyway."

A man named Brad wrote, "You did a good thing, and did more to help the Dems than anyone else I can think of this election. I know you're going through hell, but I think the silent majority really thinks what you did is great."

The correspondence from all over the world really moved me. I never realized how many people are touched—or hurt—by religious organizations.

In Denver, I suddenly found myself being recognized wherever I went. I would be stopped at my local grocery store and coffee shop. Some would say thank you, some would just say hello. I had people at my gym use their cell phones to take pictures of me doing my workout. People would come up to my table at lunch and say thank you. Even construction workers approached me to say they'd seen me on television.

My mug became even more popular after the *People* magazine story about Ted and me came out. "The Preacher and the Prostitute" seemed to be all over the place. A clerk at my local grocery store even asked me to autograph it.

Technically, the Denver Police Department still has an open investigation on what happened between Ted Haggard and me. Investigators even came to talk with me once. They had no warrant, however, and I haven't heard from them since. Many interviewers have said that they felt that either I or Ted or both had committed a crime.

Even though she was the second reporter I contacted about my affair with Ted, Patricia Calhoun didn't write an article until after Ted had resigned. "I got fucked by a male escort" was the opening line of her editorial. She wasn't happy about having to run a story after every other media outlet in the world had run something. She was the first, however, to reveal that Ted had bought a variety of sex toys, accessories, and DVDs at a local gay fetish store. She told me there were no hard feelings. That's just how it is in the news business, she said. A month later, in December, she made my picture the cover of her year-end Best of 2006 edition. I was Baby New Year, wearing nothing but a diaper and a top hat.

I walked into the local coffee shop one morning and out of nowhere, this man handed me his cell phone to talk with Jerry Wade, one of Ted Snowden's associates. I had no idea who Ted and Jerry were, but right there, this man offered to fly me to New York to attend the opening night of his Broadway comedy, *The Little Dog Laughed*, starring Johnny Galecki, who first gained fame as a teenager on the TV show *Roseanne*.

I was going to be in New York anyway to tape a television show, so I said sure. It proved to be the experience of a lifetime.

There I was standing on the red carpet along with a host of celebrities. Lisa Kudrow. Tommy Tune. Cindy Adams from Page Six of the *New York Post* was there, and she wanted some details about my relationship with Ted Haggard that I hadn't told anyone else yet. It was overwhelming, as you can imagine, but it was also wonderful. I was being treated like a celebrity.

As I watched the play, I noticed the similarities between the show and my life. Johnny Galecki, who played the male escort, charged his clients two hundred dollars a session. There was a reference to an unseen character named Arthur. The term rent boy was used in the play, and I used to advertise on Rentboy.com. It was basically my life on stage. Thank goodness the theater lights weren't on me, or the whole world would have seen me cry. There was a cast party after the show at Planet Hollywood, and that's where I was fortunate enough to meet my current literary agent, Don Farber, and his wife, Annie.

Even walking down the streets of New York, people stopped me. Young and old, white and black. Almost all said thank you, and none were disrespectful. Some even compared me to David taking down Goliath. That's not how I would describe how I felt, but I am very happy I was embraced and not shunned by the media and its viewers. During that trip, I was also filmed as part of Dan Hunt's documentary called *FROLIC* about what happens when gay men confront and work through issues related to shame and internalized homophobia.

Also in November, I flew to Florida for a photo shoot for a David Leddick coffee-table book about male escorts. He was about to wrap up the book when my story broke. Moving quickly, he called me and asked if I would come down to Florida for a nice winter vacation and spend a few hours posing for his book. I jumped on the opportunity to get away and relax for a few days. It was enjoyable and rewarding.

After my story broke, almost all my income dried up. Understandably, all the married men who saw me for massage stopped calling, fearful that they would be falsely exposed. But the rest of my regular massage and weight-training clients stopped calling, too. I understand their hesitancy, but I was taken aback when the Colorado Art Institute no longer wanted me to model for their classes. At one point in November, I was not sure how I would pay my December bills, much less have money for the Christmas season. Rumors that I would be evicted circulated as well.

Joe Jervis of JoeMyGod.blogspot.com writes a popular blog from his New York apartment. Hearing of my financial distress, he organized an online campaign whereby people could send me money via a PayPal account. His premise was simple: Mike brought down one of the most powerful antigay preachers in the world, and now he needs help. Within days, Dan Savage had posted it on his Savage Love column at the Seattle newspaper *The Stranger*, and people sent me enough money to cover my December bills, like rent and telephone. In addition, I was deemed Queer of the Year by his readers. I also was one of *The Advocate*'s People of the Year for 2006.

Long after the holidays, people still sent me money, along with personal notes, many of which were deeply moving.

I received fifty dollars from Ken of New York City, who wrote, "Please accept this modest offering as my way of saying thank you so much for doing what you did. I can't imagine the amount of courage it took for you to do so."

Susan of California, who sent me ten dollars, wrote, "Thank you so much. I'm sure your brave action was a contributing factor to the Republicans losing the House and Senate."

Shortly after that, I was able to sign a deal with Seven Stories Press to produce the book you are now reading.

All the wonderful e-mails and calls I received were from individuals who took the time and effort to tell me how they felt about me, and it was nothing short of wonderful. Yet I found it ironic and a bit sad that no gay organizations tried to contact me. I could have used some help, to be sure. I would have loved to have heard from the Human Rights Campaign or other gay groups. When I tried to make contact with them, I was snubbed. Perhaps I would have been treated differently if I had been something more "legitimate" than an escort.

Things changed in December, when the National Gay and Lesbian Task Force called to ask if I would be their guest of honor at a small fund-raiser in a private home in New York. I accepted the offer, thankful that at least one gay group was reaching out to me. I got the chance to tell my story to a small group of lesbians and gays, something I'd still like to do today. That night, they pulled in 150 people, more than triple the number that had attended last year's function. By taking a risk, it paid off handsomely for NGLTF. I was happy to do my part, and I got to visit New York again.

As I started writing more, I became more curious about the church that Ted Haggard built. Despite many friends' sincere concern for my safety, I drove down to New Life for a visit in late January 2007. I had let the pastors know that I would be coming. I went by myself.

As I drove, my mind started to wander. How would they react to me? Would they ignore me? Would they say hateful things to me? Would they be welcoming? I really had no idea what I might encounter, but if anyone thought I was going to hide or be afraid, they did not know me.

I arrived around eight on a Sunday morning, just before their nine o'clock service. I was not expected until around 8:45, so I waited in my car for a few minutes before deciding to get up and stroll around the grounds. I walked over to the World Prayer Center, where a huge spinning globe greeted me inside. Nothing really stood out except a couple of paintings

I saw as homoerotic. A few people passed by, but no one seemed to recognize me.

It was half an hour before the service, so I made my way to the main entrance of the church. As I approached, I could see a few heads turn, but I pretended that I didn't notice and headed for the bookstore, which was immediately inside the entrance. I could find none of Ted Haggard's books for sale. In fact, I could not find any reference to Ted whatsoever.

As the crowd grew, one by one, people started to recognize my face. I was prepared for just about anything, including venom. Instead, people began to approach me to say hello and to shake my hand. And to my surprise, they were saying thank you. The most frequent comment I heard was, "Thank you, Mike, for exposing the deception that we were experiencing for so many years." I was taken aback and said you're welcome. Many ended the conversation by saying, "God bless you."

I took a seat inside the arena before the service started. It felt more like a rock concert, with loud music coming from a band—yes, a band—on a circular stage right in the middle of the arena. Everything was a production, and it was very high tech. I felt like I was anywhere but at a religious service.

Toward the end of the service, or show, one of the pastors told the faithful, "We have been rocked with scandal, and we are overcoming it, but again what we have learned is that we cannot believe everything that comes out of one man's mouth. The only person you can truly believe is Jesus Christ."

I met Pastor Rob Brendle in the foyer, where he told me, "Mike, I don't want to impose my religious beliefs on you, but I believe God used you to correct us, and I appreciate that."

As impressive as New Life Church is, I felt that something

was missing. It's a big place, almost like a city within a city. If the gospel truly is the drawing card, why the big lavish productions?

Many have asked me if I felt that the people I met there were sincere with me. I believe they were.

Also in late January, the HBO documentary *Friends of God* debuted. Filmed and edited before the 2006 elections, the movie was written, directed, and produced by Alexandra Pelosi, daughter of U.S. Speaker of the House Nancy Pelosi, and it features Ted Haggard prominently. This was the show where Ted infamously proclaimed that "evangelicals have the best sex lives." Pelosi complained that Ted's fall caused problems for her documentary, but I think it helped her documentary attract viewers.

Ted emerged from his reparative therapy—yes, that is what it's called —in early February 2007. When the process was completed (who knows how that's determined), Ted emerged "completely heterosexual," according to church overseers.

Sensing how badly that bit of publicity went for Haggard, New Life Church announced shortly afterward that they had reached an agreement with the Haggards. The family agreed to move from Colorado and break all ties with New Life Church, all for an undisclosed sum of money. Ted also agreed never to talk again about what had happened between him and me, so unless he decides to break that agreement, we may never know what he was thinking or feeling.

Ever since my story broke, my life changed. This story had a much bigger impact than I, or anyone, could have imagined. My only goal was to expose Ted Haggard's hypocrisy. In the process, I showed that one person *can* make a difference. It just takes courage.

I can honestly tell you that I have no regrets. I did the best I could at that moment in time. Looking back, would I have done things differently? Perhaps, but I gain nothing by dwelling on the past, wondering "what if."

It's odd to be called a liar one day and a hero the next. I am not angry at the people who have said nasty or hurtful things about me. My story may be hard for some people to comprehend. It's all right to disagree with other people and how they live, but please do not judge too harshly. As my story points out, we all have plenty of baggage in life—and we all deserve happiness and equal rights.